To: ...

Love from: Grandpa Jim
&
"Grandma Julie"

ANNIE'S SONG

By Betsy Corona

Copyright © 2009 by Betsy Corona

Annie's Song
by Betsy Corona

Printed in the United States of America

ISBN 978-1-60791-370-2

All rights reserved solely by the author. The author guarantees all contents are original and do not infringe upon the legal rights of any other person or work. No part of this book may be reproduced in any form without the permission of the author. The views expressed in this book are not necessarily those of the publisher.

www.xulonpress.com

ACKNOWLEDGMENTS

Thanks and praise go to God Almighty for the inspiration, energy, and resources He gave me to bring Emma and Annie to life.

Many thanks go to Melissa Bogdany, my wonderful editor, who refined *Annie's Song* in order to make it "sing."

Thanks and appreciation go to Tracy Sullivan, my first contact with Xulon Press, for her kindness and patience.

Love and gratitude go to my dear niece and godchild, Kara Thompson, for her beautiful artwork that graces the cover of *Annie's Song*.

Warm thanks go to my husband, Rick, who gave me all kinds of support while I worked on my manuscript.

DEDICATION

This book is dedicated to all the Annies of the world. May their special qualities continue to help transform all those willing to connect with them.

TABLE OF CONTENTS

CHAPTER ONE: GETTING TO KNOW YOU
After meeting Annie, Emma tries to share her world,
but Annie doesn't respond. 11

CHAPTER TWO: SOMETHING SPECIAL
Emma's mother tries to explain why Annie
is so different. 23

CHAPTER THREE: A DIFFERENT WORLD
Emma is amazed by how different Annie's home
is from her own. 29

CHAPTER FOUR: WHERE TO FIND PATIENCE
Emma learns that there is a price to pay
for friendship with Annie. 37

CHAPTER FIVE: MAKING PROGRESS
Emma's efforts start to pay off. 43

CHAPTER SIX: LONGING TO BELONG
Nona Lisa reminds Emma that Annie just
wants to feel like she belongs. 49

CHAPTER SEVEN: WHAT TO DO?
Emma feels lost with Annie gone. 55

CHAPTER EIGHT: A REVELATION
The beauty of the girls' friendship comes to life
right in the Moreaus' living room. 59

CHAPTER NINE: A MOUNTAIN AND A MOLE HILL
The school year brings conflicts for Emma. 71

CHAPTER TEN: FACING HER FEARS
Keeping the friendship going takes its toll,
but Emma's mother encourages her to press on................77

CHAPTER ELEVEN: MORE PROGRESS
Rosalie notices changes in Emma.....................................87

CHAPTER TWELVE: MORE CHALLENGES
Emma goes out on a limb for Angela................................95

CHAPTER THIRTEEN: HELPING OUT
Rosalie and Emma have a heart-to-heart. 103

CHAPTER FOURTEEN: LIKE ONE OF THE FAMILY
Emma and Annie now feel like family............................111

CHAPTER FIFTEEN: THE GIFT OPENED
On Christmas Eve, Emma realizes the best
gifts don't come with bows...121

CHAPTER ONE

GETTING TO KNOW YOU

Gifts can come in all kinds of packages. Some are pretty; some are not. Some have bows and fancy paper; some don't. Why, you just might have to ponder some awhile just to figure out if they really are gifts! This might take some time, and it might take some patience, too.

A gift like that showed up one hot June day back in 1957. It arrived on Oxford Road, a pretty suburban street. The branches of the giant elms swayed in the breeze, chasing the sparrows all the way down to the lake. Yes, it was a perfect day for a gift, you might say. But Emma Palermo didn't seem to think so, for the gift was sitting right across the street from her house, just waiting to be discovered. And Emma, why, Emma was in no mood for presents that morning. Seems she was too busy arguing with her mother to notice anything. And don't you know, she almost missed it.

"Man, oh, man! I can't do that, Mother!" Emma wailed.

"Yes, you can, dear," her mother replied.

"Oh, I just can't walk up to some stranger and start talking like some nerd! Send Rosalie, please!"

"Rosie and Angie are busy cleaning out their closets, and besides, that little girl is not a stranger; she's our brand new neighbor, and she looks like your age. Those boys over there are probably her brothers, but they are just ignoring her."

Mrs. Palermo and her youngest daughter, Emma, were peeking out their living room window at the scene across the street. A new family had moved in the day before. Now, the boys were busy tossing a football around their front yard, and a girl who seemed to be their younger sister sat watching from the sidelines.

Luckily, the air conditioner was on and the windows were closed at Emma's house, so no one outside could hear the debate going on between ten-year-old Emma and her mother.

"She looks weird to me," Emma protested.

"Emma, stop that now! That is so unkind of you! Her hair is just in curlers. That's not weird. She looks lonely, though, and you could help with that."

Placing a hand on her daughter's shoulder, Mrs. Palermo tried to see what Emma was wearing.

"Ooooo!" Emma whined.

"Oh, stop! I just want to see how you look before I send you over there, young lady. When did you put these Bermuda shorts on?"

"Yesterday." Emma fidgeted some more. "I'll feel dumb walking over there! Why don't you go, Mother?" Emma winced as her mother tried to arrange Emma's long, curly hair.

"Why, I have a lasagna to take over in the oven right now, but it isn't ready yet. So you go and introduce yourself, and see if she would like to come in out of the heat for some lemonade."

"Oh, man, do I have to?" Emma knew she was stuck, but she wasn't finished complaining.

"Yes, you have to. Go on, now, and be nice. I have things to do."

Her mother tried to give Emma a hug, but Emma would have none of it. Shrugging away, she headed for their front door, yanked it open, and lurched out onto the sun-filled porch. She knew better than to slam the door. So she just stood there, eyeing the activity across the street. She was aware of the fact that her mother was watching her just stand there, but she didn't care.

Looking down, she thrust her hands into the pockets of her shorts. They were a little wrinkled. Frowning, she stared at her PF Flyers. Oh, how she loved her new sneakers! They were so white.

Looking up now at her new neighbors, she sighed. *Man, oh, man, what am I going to say to her?* Emma was fretting. She knew she had a problem. In fact, she had a couple of problems. For one, she hated talking to strangers, girls or boys, but especially boys. And two, she really didn't want another female in her life, thank you very much. Her little world had enough women in it already: her mother, her Nona Lisa, and her sisters, Rosalie and Angela. She certainly didn't need any more to tell her what to do! Thank God for her father, Frank. "Father wouldn't make me go," she mumbled as she kicked a stone into the bushes. "He'd get me out of this."

Frank Palermo wouldn't be home for another five hours, so she knew she had to get moving. Slowly, she began her march down the long, U-shaped driveway. When she reached the curb, she stopped, but the ball-playing across the way continued. And the little girl did not move.

Oh, man, do I have to go all the way over there? Emma let out a moan. Feeling foolish, but not knowing what else to do, she began to wave at the little blonde twenty feet away. Emma did her best to get the girl's attention, but Emma only seemed to catch the eye of the four boys. When they saw her, they stopped and stared.

Oh, man, they stopped their game! Emma panicked. *No, no, not you fellas, your sister!* Emma was caught. There was no place to hide. *Now what do I do?* The little girl came to her rescue.

When she saw Emma, the young neighbor got up and started walking toward the street. But before crossing, she paused and looked over her shoulder at the tallest of the brothers. He nodded "okay," and she proceeded.

Oh, here she comes! Emma turned her head to see if her mother was still watching. Mrs. Palermo waved her daughter on and then disappeared behind the drapes. As the little girl came closer, Emma noticed a few things about her. She looked to be about the same height as Emma. She wore a pair of linen shorts and a dainty, gold charm bracelet. *She isn't very pretty.*

Maybe it's the curlers, Emma thought. She remembered her mother's words about being kind, and so she looked at the girl and smiled.

"Hi, I'm Emma," she said.

"I'm Anne," the girl replied.

She's got braces on her teeth! Man! Emma realized she was staring, but she couldn't help herself. Anne had sad, brown eyes that held little expression. *What do I say now?* Then it came to Emma. "My mother wants to know if you want to come in and play." There, she had done it!

Without saying a word or smiling, Anne started toward the Palermos' front door. Emma walked beside her and escorted her inside.

The aroma of Emma's mother's lasagna greeted the girls as they entered the cool, marble foyer. Emma brought Anne to the kitchen. Emma got out the lemonade her mother had mentioned and went to see if there were any cookies around, even if they were store-bought. The Palermos, you see, were not known for their baking, but, oh, could they cook!

Emma climbed a chair and brought down her favorite striped glasses. She made the lemonade every afternoon for her father. He loved to drink it when he came home from work all hot and thirsty. Emma felt proud to pour some now from the big glass pitcher for her company. Anne waited at the kitchen table.

And there they sat, drinking and munching their Oreos in silence. Emma, not having much of a social life outside of her family, wasn't used to entertaining. *Okay, now what do I do with her? What do I say?* she worried. Then she remembered what her relatives always seemed to ask her at the holidays.

"What grade are you in?" she asked Anne. Anne looked up from her cookies and politely swallowed before answering. "I go to the Convent school. Fourth Grade." Emma knew of the exclusive Convent of the Sacred Heart on the lake because it was right next door to her school.

"Oh, that's great. I go to St. Paul's. I'll be in fifth grade. I turn ten in three weeks. You must be nine." Anne looked down at her plate and frowned. "No, I'm ten, too. My birthday was in May." She pushed her plate away from her.

Oh, man! What did I say? She looks like she's going to cry! Emma freaked. She got up to carry the dishes to the sink. Her feelings of panic rose. *Oh, I'm not doing so well. Mother will kill me if she cries!*

Just at that moment, Emma's mother swept into the room. "Well, I see we have a guest, Emma. How nice. Are you going to introduce me?" asked her mother. Emma sighed with relief, but she didn't move from the sink. "Oh, Mother, this is Annie."

"Hello, Annie. I'm Mrs. Palermo. Welcome to our neighborhood."

"Hello," Anne said, with her eyes fixed on the table.

"I have something in the oven for your family and would like to bring it over later on. Is your mother at home unpacking?"

Anne looked up, confused. Cooking and unpacking boxes were two things her mother did not do. "Mother's not at home, but Madelaine is."

"Oh, and who is Madelaine?" Emma's mother asked. Her question was innocent enough.

"She's our cook," Anne replied.

Emma shot a glance at her mother. *They have a cook?* In Emma's world, you were usually related to the cook. Then Anne volunteered more.

"Mary's home, too."

"And Mary is . . .?"

"Mary's our maid. And Hans is our butler. He drives Mother places, too."

This was too much for Emma. She went to her mother's side and grabbed her hand. Mrs. Palermo gulped, but she didn't miss a beat. "Well, it sounds like you have a really full house over there, dear. I'm so glad I made an extra large lasagna!" *Way to go, Mother! Mother always knows what to say!* Emma cheered to herself. But she was floored by what she had just heard.

Maids and butlers right across the street? And chauffeurs? Across from the Palermos'? Emma had every reason to love her beautiful home, with its many baths and bedrooms. Father had taken such care to build it, and Mother had taken such pride in furnishing it. Why, it had all the modern conveniences and more, but . . . no servants—unless you were counting faithful Mrs. Fromm, the sweet German lady who came to clean every Tuesday and Friday, rain or shine. But even with Mrs. Fromm, there were always household chores that needed to be done, and every member of the Palermo family was expected to help out.

The home across the street was in a league all its own. This grand old Tudor mansion had servants' quarters above the garage. It reminded Emma, who loved anything to do with movie pictures, of the movie *Sabrina*, starring Audrey Hepburn. Emma started to get excited thinking about the possibility of exploring the world over there. But her mother brought her back to earth.

"Emma, why don't you take Annie up to your room and show her around? Maybe she would like to borrow a few of your Nancy Drews."

Emma frowned at the thought. *Share my books?* But then, another terrible thought took its place. *My room! How did I leave it this morning? She doesn't want to see my old room. Hers is probably enormous.*

Anne stared at Emma and waited. Emma stared back. *What else can I do with her? She sure doesn't talk much.* "Okay, Annie, come on, we'll go upstairs." Emma turned and walked toward the back staircase. "We can go see what my sisters are up to."

A few minutes later, they reached Emma's bedroom. "Here we are," Emma announced as she led the way. She gave the room a quick once-over. She had to admit, it was a very pretty room, even if a bit messy. The attached sundeck made it truly unique. Emma's sisters loved to sunbathe there.

Inside, though, tiny rosebuds danced all over the twin, taffeta bedspreads. Her small desk had a key for its drawer, so Emma could keep her diary from prying eyes. The matching bookcase was the home for her Madame Alexander dolls and, of course, her beloved books.

"Do you like Nancy Drew?" Emma asked, picking up a stray pajama top and tossing it on a chair. Silence. She pulled a copy of *The Haunted Bridge* from the bookcase and turned to face Anne, standing in the doorway.

"I don't read much," Anne said, looking around the room. Emma looked down at the book—a dead end.

"Well, what do you do for fun?" Emma wasn't about to drag out her doll collection.

"I have a horse," Anne replied in a quiet voice.

Emma's jaw dropped. *Man, oh, man, she has a horse? Her own horse?* She was shocked, but she knew she could not act jealous. "Wow, that's so cool! What's its name?" Emma put the book back on its shelf.

"His name is King. Larry's horse is Lil'bit." Even as she spoke of her pets, Anne's face showed little expression.

But Emma's eyes were practically popping out of their sockets in disbelief. "Who is Larry?"

"He's one of my brothers. We ride at the Hunt Club." Anne said all of this in a very matter-of-fact tone.

It was all too much for Emma. She had to sit down. *Not one horse in the family, but two! And I thought she might want to play with my dolls! How dumb! No wonder she looks so bored.* Emma sat and stared at the floor.

Anne sat down now on the other bed. "What's wrong?" she asked.

Emma looked up and laughed. She was at a loss for words. *How am I supposed to entertain someone who has her own horse?* She shook her head. "Nothing is wrong, Annie. Everything is just hunky-dory." But in truth, she was stumped. Then an idea popped into her head. "Let's go find my sisters," she exclaimed as she jumped up and trotted from the room.

Emma had two beautiful dark-haired sisters. They were tall and willowy, just like their mother. Emma hoped and prayed that she would grow up someday to look like them. She envied them, with their high-heeled pumps and their nylon stockings and their long, full skirts with their crinoline slips. Both girls were allowed to drive their mother's

Chrysler station wagon, and they were both very smart and did well in school.

"You'll like them, Annie. They have cool stuff in their rooms." They were standing in the middle of the upstairs hall. Emma called out. "Rosie, Angela, where are you?"

"We're in here, and stop calling me Rosie," Rosalie answered. Emma headed toward the doorway on the left. Anne stayed right behind her.

"Hi, what are you guys doing?" Emma asked, surveying the clutter. There were shoes, hatboxes, and piles of clothing all around the room.

"Well, what does it look like we're doing, silly? We're cleaning out closets." Rosalie was bent over a stack of wool sweaters with her hair covering her eyes. Angela had her back to the girls as she arranged skirts and blouses in the closet. Finally, Rosalie noticed two sets of feet in her doorway and looked up to ask. "Who's your friend?"

Emma turned around and pulled Anne into view. "This is Annie, our neighbor across the street. Annie, these are my two sisters, Rosalie, and Angela is over there in the closet."

Angela looked over her shoulder, pausing only a moment to greet her. "Hi, Annie. Come on in, but watch where you step. Welcome to our mess."

"We have a lot of mess at our house, too," Anne said, remaining in the doorway.

Emma was excited to fill her sisters in about their new neighbor. "Annie has four brothers and a horse—one is named Larry."

Rosalie stood up now and placed her hands on her hips. "You have a horse named Larry? Really?" she asked, pretending to be confused.

Emma, anxious to explain, continued her riddle. "No, one of her brothers is Larry. The horse is named King! Larry has a horse, too, named Lil'bit, and she's going to the Convent."

It was Angela's turn to stop now. The older sisters looked at each other and howled. "Ha, ha, ha, ha, ha." "I don't think the good Sisters allow horses at the Convent," Angela teased.

Emma moaned. "Ohhhhh." When she got excited, she would often jumble her pronouns, and her sisters loved to joke with her about it. "You guys know what I mean," Emma sighed.

"How nice for you, Annie. You'll like the Convent. I know some girls who went there, and they really enjoyed it," Rosalie said, returning to her work.

Emma looked at them. She was surprised that all this information about their new neighbors failed to impress her sisters more.

"So what are you two going to do today? Going swimming?" Angela asked.

"No. Mother has too much work to do," Emma said, as she sidled up to Rosalie's vanity. Emma loved this whole room, but one piece of furniture in particular held her interest, and that was Rosalie's antique dressing table. Emma thought it to be a magical shrine where you sat and gazed into its lovely, etched mirror and somehow were transformed into a fairy princess! Anne caught Emma's gaze and went over to see what had captured Emma's attention.

In the middle of the vanity, on a dainty glass tray, sat Rosalie's fabulous perfume bottles. She had been collecting them for years, and Emma loved arranging them, sampling them, and just plain looking at all the shapes and colors. They twinkled in the daylight as Emma reached for her favorite—Evening in Paris—a deep, cobalt blue crystal.

"Aren't these great, Annie?" Emma's voice was full of admiration, and she hoped that Anne would like them, too. But Anne just stared at the dazzling array. Her face showed no emotion.

"Can we try some, Rosalie, please?" Emma begged, and without waiting for permission, she gave herself a little squirt on the wrist.

"Mother has a table like this," Anne said, her voice perfectly flat. Emma couldn't tell if Anne liked them or not. *Boy, she's funny. But then probably everything is bigger and better over at her house,* Emma sighed, returning the bottle to its place on the tray. Emma was sure her sister's collection would be a big hit.

Rosalie noticed her sister's look of disappointment and came over to give Emma a hug. "I have an idea. Why don't you two go downstairs and listen to some records? Do you like Pat Boone, Annie?" Anne nodded. "Great, 'cause, you see, Angie and I have to clean up this room, and Emma has some great Pat Boone records. So you two scoot now, okay? It sure was nice meeting you."

"Come back and visit soon," Angela called from the closet.

Emma smiled and headed for the door. She was so grateful for her sister's suggestion. She would take Anne to the basement, where it was sure to be cool, and they could play *Bernadine* as loudly as they pleased!

CHAPTER TWO

SOMETHING SPECIAL

Emma considered her first attempts at a social life a disaster. Her ten-year-old brain just couldn't understand why Anne acted the way she did. Emma thought about this a lot at dinner that night while she pushed her food around on her plate. *She almost cried over her cookies, and she didn't seem to like my room or even Nancy Drew! She just stared at Rosalie's beautiful bottles. The only thing she seemed to like all day was Pat Boone, and we had to cut that short 'cause Father came home. Man! I just have to ask Mother what to do.* After the dishes were done, she got her chance. It was time to get her hair washed.

"Ouch, that hurts!" Emma cried as her mother worked the shampoo into Emma's long curls. It had been a long day, and her mother was tired. She wanted this one last chore to be over. "Stop wiggling, young lady. I don't want water on the floor."

"Where's the rag? I'm getting soap in my eyes. Oh, man!"

"It's on your left, dear, on the towel bar. We're going to rinse now, so cover up." Her mother reached for the red aluminum glass and began to pour warm water over the soapy head. She was so glad she no longer had to do this for Rosalie or Angela.

"Mother, I don't understand something."

"What is it, dear?"

Emma blotted her eyes with the washrag. "OOOOO, man! It's still in my eyes. This rag is all wet." Emma wiggled and stamped her feet. Mrs. Palermo grabbed a dry rag and traded with her daughter.

"There, is that better? Hang on, we're almost done." And she blew a wisp of her own, graying hair out of her face as she continued to rinse. "What don't you understand?" She hoped this would not take too long.

"I don't understand Annie. I know she's my age, but she's not like me at all. She didn't seem to like any of my stuff today. Man, she didn't even like Rosalie's perfume collection. Everybody likes that! And she never smiled the whole afternoon. Why do you think she's like that?"

Emma's mother started to dry Emma's head, taking her time to answer her daughter. She handed Emma the comb and brush and sat down on the edge of the bathtub. Emma remained at the sink, combing out her wet hair.

"Annie is," she paused, "different from you, Emma. God made her in a special way."

Emma frowned. "What do you mean, different? 'Cause she owns a horse?"

"No, no, my dear." Mrs. Palermo smiled as she looked down at her hands, folded in her lap. She sighed. This was not going to be easy to explain. "No, Emma, the horse and servants and all that is not what I mean. Annie is just," she paused again, "slow." She looked up to catch her daughter's reaction. Emma looked confused.

"Slow at what? We didn't do any running today, and besides, she told me that she isn't allowed to run outside. Isn't that silly?" Emma put the comb down and folded her arms, waiting for more.

Her mother looked out the bathroom window. *How can I say this so she understands?* she wondered. *Dear God, please help me here.* "It's just that God didn't make Annie like He made you or Rosalie or Angela."

"Man, you can say that again!" Emma said, still frowning.

"I don't mean physically, dear. I mean mentally. Mentally, Annie is a bit slow at catching on to things."

"Man, do I know that! I tried to teach her a dance step while we listened to Pat Boone, and she just couldn't get it. It was an easy step, too!"

"It might be easy for you, dear, but not for her. Most of the things you do, dear, are not going to be easy for someone like Annie."

"You mean there's more than one like her? I thought you said she was special?"

"She is special, and she's unique, just like you and your sisters are unique. But you three girls are quick and smart, and Annie is not. So you are going to have to find lots of patience, Emma, if you want to be friends with Annie. She has great qualities, too. It's just going to take you some time to discover and appreciate them."

"Well, if Annie doesn't catch on so fast, how can she go to the Convent in the fall?" Emma's eyes suddenly lit up. She remembered what Annie had said in the kitchen. "Oh, man, maybe that's why Annie isn't going into the fifth grade like I am, even though she's ten!"

"Exactly. Annie needs extra help," Emma's mother replied.

"But the Convent school is supposed to be hard, Mother." Emma still wasn't getting it.

"But the Convent has small classes, remember, and the Sisters have the time to give Annie the extra help she needs. Why, maybe you can go over there and help her a little with her homework sometime." Mrs. Palermo stopped. She hoped that this was enough information for the moment. She stood up, yawning. "Come on, let's get that hair of yours in some curlers before bed."

"Oh, please, please, please, Mother, let me try doing my own hair. I've watched the girls so many times. Please?"

Irene Palermo smiled, grabbed the bag of brown rubber curlers from under the sink, and handed them over. "Be my guest."

Emma saw Anne three days later at Sunday mass. It was a glorious day, with Lake St. Clair sparkling in the sun and the stained glass of old St. Paul's church bursting with life. The bells began to toll as Frank Palermo led his family inside to their usual pew.

"Why do we always have to sit in the back?" Emma grumbled to herself as she followed her sisters. She was wearing her pretty Easter dress, the one that made her feel like Princess Margaret, and she wanted the whole world to see. She knelt down, but instead of praying, she fussed with her little straw hat. Catching a frown from her mother, she sat back and proceeded to remove her gloves. She had no place to put them. *I have to start bringing a purse. But what do you put in a purse besides handkerchiefs and gloves?* She looked down the pew at Rosalie's and Angela's purses. *Keys! Maybe Mother will give me my very own house key.* She was lost in these thoughts when she spotted Anne.

The entire Moreau family was making their way down the long aisle toward the front pews. Anne, wearing a pink sundress, was holding her pretty, blonde mother's hand. Mr. Moreau was right behind them in a dark suit, and he was followed by the four boys, well-scrubbed in their polo shirts.

Emma shot a quick glance at her sisters to see if they were looking at Anne's brothers. *I wonder if they think they're cute.* Nona Lisa and Emma's mother were praying with their eyes cast down, and Emma's father was staring straight ahead, but Rosalie and Angela saw what she saw. Emma smiled, quite pleased with herself.

But during the sermon, she got bored. She gazed up at the giant marble statue of Jesus in the sanctuary and figured that this was a good time to talk to God about Anne. She closed her eyes, folded her hands, and prayed. *Dear God, I know You don't owe me an explanation or anything, but could You tell me why You made Annie the way You did? Could You send me a clue? Her brothers look nice and happy, and she always looks so sad. Please, Lord, help me to know how to play with her. I'm not good at jokes like Rosalie, so how can I get her to laugh? Please send me more information. Amen.*

The priest finished his talk, so Emma took out her blue hymnal. All the Palermos were strong singers, but Emma's voice stood out from the rest. She had been singing with Doris Day, Pat Boone, and Perry Como since she was a little girl, hadn't she? She felt confident carrying a tune. This was her talent, and today, especially, she wanted God to hear!

CHAPTER THREE

A DIFFERENT WORLD

The next day was wash day. Even though Mrs. Fromm came to polish and vacuum, the Palermo girls pitched in with various chores on hot summer days so Mrs. Fromm could go home early.

Emma didn't mind. She loved Mrs. Fromm, and today she even liked some of her tasks. Today she would collect all the small area rugs around the house, take them to her sundeck, and give them a good shaking over the railing there. She was in the middle of doing this when she spotted a black sedan driving up the Moreaus' front drive. Anne and one of her brothers got out. The Cadillac then backed up and drove off. Emma knew her mother would not approve of Emma's yelling, but she couldn't resist the urge, and so she called out at the top of her lungs.

"Helloooooo there," she called, waving wildly to get Anne's attention—not one bit shy like a few days before.

Anne turned and looked around to see who was calling, blocking her eyes from the sun with her arm. She caught sight of Emma, high on the sundeck, and waved back. Then she followed her brother into the house.

As Emma smiled and went back to her rugs, she realized what she was wearing. *Oh, man, what will she think! Here I* am in a housecoat, shaking out rugs! Bet she doesn't do this kind of stuff at her house. She's got Mary and Madelaine. Oh, man. She let out a big sigh as she gathered up her piles and disappeared through the sundeck door. Even though she heard the phone ringing, she ignored it. It was never for her, so she finished her task and carried the rugs to their various rooms. Then she heard her mother's voice.

"Oh, Emma," her mother called from the stairway, "please pick up the phone."

Surprised, Emma dropped the rugs and ran to her mother and father's bedroom for the nearest extension. She tried to be careful about the way she sat on her father's bed. She crossed her legs and picked up the receiver the way she had seen her sisters often do. She wanted to act casual about the whole thing, but she was too excited.

"Hello," Emma said in a soft voice.

"Hello, this is Anne. Do you want to play at my house today?" Anne asked.

"I have to ask my mother," Emma said, thinking of the chores still left undone. "Maybe I can come this afternoon, after lunch. Is that okay?" Emma hoped with all her heart that it was okay. She was just dying to see Anne's house.

"You can call me back. This is my number," Anne answered.

"Oh, wait. I have to find a pencil." Emma tore through the nightstand. *Where do they keep these things? Man, I am so uncool.* But she finally located a pad and pen. "Ready."

"It's Tuxedo 6-0407."

"60407," Emma repeated. "How did you know my number?"

"Madelaine looked it up for me."

Of course she did! What was I thinking? Emma sighed before answering, "I'll ask my mother and call you back, okay?" After Anne said good-bye, Emma sat on the bed and stared at the receiver for a moment before replacing it. Then she got up to assess the damage to the bed. After smoothing the beautiful brocade to her satisfaction, she happily thought about her "date" and went in search of her mother.

"Mother," she yelled as she fairly flew down the winding front staircase. The white-carpeted front stairs were off limits to Emma as a rule, but today—today was the dawn of her social life, and she couldn't find her mother fast enough!

"Emma, stop your hollering, please, and come find me. I'm in the den," her mother said in a stern voice.

"Man, oh, man, that was Annie on the phone, and she wants me to play at her house after lunch." She was panting as she reached her mother, who was writing out bills at her big leather-topped desk. "Is that okay? I have to call her back. Here, she gave me her number." Emma showed the scrap of paper to her mother, not knowing what else to do with it.

"Calm down, child," Mrs. Palermo laughed as she turned to her daughter. "Yes, you can go if your jobs are done. Are they?"

"Oh, man," Emma said, frowning. "I finished everything but the shoes!" Emma was the official shoe-polishing expert in the family. She did it willingly and with great care, but today, shoes were the last thing she wanted to think about.

"Oh, I guess your father can wait another day for those brown oxfords, and I certainly don't want you to hurry with my spectator pumps, either, so I guess you can do them later. But please, Emma, go take a bath and put on some clean clothes, for heaven's sake!"

Emma gave her mother a quick kiss, then raced from the room, singing, "Hot diggity, dog ziggity, boom, what you do to me . . ." at the top of her lungs. Perry Como would be proud.

For the second time in a week, Emma marched down her front drive, leading to the Moreau mansion. She was no longer afraid. In fact, she had to keep herself from skipping right into the street. Oxford Road was such a quiet street that Emma was allowed to cross on her own. As Emma approached the big Tudor, she marveled at all the windows and wondered which one might be Anne's room. Today, she knew she was "company." *Should I use their front door?* It looked so forbidding! It looked like one from a haunted house movie where Vincent Price or Peter Lorre playing the butler greeted you in their creepy fashion. *No, I think I'll use the side door Annie used this morning. It looks a lot friendlier.* So Emma climbed the two steps, lifted the heavy knocker, and knocked.

When that door opened, Emma's life changed forever. She entered a very different world, and somehow she knew this. She was so excited to see what it had to offer. Her heart pounded as her curiosity propelled her forward.

"Well, hello there, Miss. Who might you be, and how might I help you?" A pleasant-looking grey-haired woman answered the door. She smiled down at Emma.

"I'm Emma from across the street," Emma explained in a shaky voice. "Annie is expecting me." *This must be Madelaine or Mary,* she thought, noticing the uniform and apron. The woman had rosy cheeks and wore glasses. *She looks just like Mrs. Claus!*

"Well, Emma from across the street, isn't that nice?" the woman said. "Miss Anne is up in her room. Come in now, and I'll take you to her. My name is Mary, by the way." Her warm manner put Emma at ease. She followed Mary down a short hallway, past a breakfast room, and into a large kitchen. Mary stopped at the stove to speak to a woman peering into a large pot.

"Emma, this here lady is Madelaine, our wonderful cook. Madelaine, this is Emma from across the street, here to visit Miss Anne."

Madelaine was a very pretty woman with dimples. She stopped her stirring and smiled at Emma. "Oooooooo, *chérie*, how sweet you are to come!"

Emma couldn't help but smile back. *Man! She has a French accent! Wait 'til I tell Rosalie and Angela!* Emma was intrigued.

"I hope you enjoy your *vizeet*," Madelaine continued, "and I hope that you come often." (No one had any idea just how often Emma would visit.) "Now, *excusez-moi*, but I have to rescue my bouillabaisse!" And she frowned into the pot.

Emma had no clue what Madelaine meant, but Emma loved hearing French spoken in such a musical way. Mary, however, was marching through the kitchen door, and Emma had to scurry to catch up.

They entered the great front hall, which was dim, with just a few rays of light shining through the tall staircase windows. *Wow! This is like the movie Rebecca.* At the far end of the hall, you could see the Moreau living rooms, quiet and mysterious. *I feel like I'm in a castle!* Emma paused, taking in the grandeur of the high ceilings, the deep aqua carpeting, and the huge crystal chandelier twinkling from above. *Man, this sure is a beautiful house, but how can we play in a place like this?* Emma wondered as they climbed the stairs in silence. When they reached the top, an antique needlepoint settee greeted them. It sat right next to Anne's door.

"There you go, dear; she's right in there," Mary said, pointing at the door. Go on in now and enjoy yourselves."

She must be joking! Emma thought as she smiled and said, "Thank you." She walked toward the door and gave it a little shove. It was heavy, so she shoved it again.

"Hello?" she called in a tiny voice. "Annie, are you in here?" She walked through an entrance with closets on the sides. It opened up to a lovely room, which was huge, just like Emma thought it would be. Emma stopped and stared. She wanted to remember it all so she could report back to her sisters.

Butterflies. The pale green room was covered with butterflies! They were everywhere—on the walls, the bedspreads, the chairs. The back wall was all windows looking out onto the back yard. The light poured in and fell on Anne's very grown-up, French provincial desk. Emma looked around the room for any sign of dolls, stuffed animals, or games. There were none. *There's no bookcase, either*, she thought. But her eyes finally did hit upon something that she recognized: a record player. *Annie has her own record player, and look at that stack of albums!* She started to cross the room to see them when she stopped. *Where is Annie?* She called out again.

"Annie, it's Emma. Are you in here?"

"Yes," came her muffled reply. "I'm trying to fix my hair."

Emma followed the sound, which came from a door on her right. *A bathroom! Annie has her own bathroom!* She went and rapped on the door. "Do you want some help?"

Anne opened the door. Her hair was a fright, so Emma went right to work. Emma's own curly hair turned to frizz every summer, and ponytails were the only possible solution.

"Thanks," Anne said when the last strand had been secured.

"You have a big record collection. Can I look through them?" Emma asked.

"Sure, but my mother wants to meet you," Anne said. "She's in her room." Anne moved past Emma, out of her room, and into the hall. Emma followed.

Mrs. Moreau's bedroom consisted of a suite of rooms you could find with your eyes closed.

"Ooooooh, what's that wonderful smell?" Emma asked as she closed her eyes and paused outside the master bedroom.

"Oh, that's mother's perfume. It's the only one she'll wear."

Emma's eyes popped back open. "Really?" She thought that half the fun of wearing perfume was all of the choices you had. "What's it called?" she asked as she found herself staring at the largest bed she had ever seen.

"Joy," Anne replied as she continued walking down the small corridor. They passed a dressing room and a bathroom before they reached their destination. The girls stood in the doorway of Mrs. Moreau's sitting room and waited for her to look up from her desk. She was in the middle of a phone call, but she smiled and beckoned them to come in.

She's so beautiful, Emma thought as they came closer. There were few blondes in the Palermo family, and Emma was captivated. Mrs. Moreau's golden, bouffant hair reminded Emma of the halos that were on the saints of her holy card collection. Anne's mother had blue eyes that matched her linen skirt. She wore a silk blouse and a gold charm bracelet with huge charms on it.

Emma just stood there, speechless. She was thinking of her own mother, in her simple housedress, right across the street.

"Well, Anne, who do we have here?" Michelle Moreau asked as she glided forward.

"This is Emma from across the street," Anne replied.

"How do you do, Emma? It's so nice of you to come for a visit." Her voice seemed to float in the air, or at least Emma thought so.

Did she just say, "How do you do" to me? Emma was floored. No one had ever spoken to her in such grown-up language before. *What do I say? Do I curtsy? What would Mother say?* After a moment, her manners came to her.

"I'm fine, thank you. You have a lovely home."

"Why, thank you, Emma. We still have a lot of pictures to hang and such, but we like it here very much. Do you girls want to watch TV up here? I have to go to Mrs. Pritchard's for a fitting."

Emma looked at Anne. She knew Anne had to decide where they played, but Emma didn't want to get stuck inside. Anne said nothing.

"Or perhaps you can take Emma out in the yard, Anne, and show her your statue," Mrs. Moreau continued.

"Oh, I would love to see your statue," Emma blurted out, not having the foggiest idea of what Mrs. Moreau meant.

"Okay," Anne said. She turned and left the room without a word of good-bye to her mother. Emma was surprised, but Mrs. Moreau did not seem phased by her daughter's abrupt behavior.

"It was nice meeting you," Emma said.

"You, too, dear . . . and oh, do thank your mother for sending over that divine lasagna. Everyone enjoyed it so! Come, I'll walk out with you." She stopped to grab her handbag. It matched her shoes, of course.

CHAPTER FOUR

WHERE TO FIND PATIENCE

~~~~~~

After the girls watched the big, black sedan drive Mrs. Moreau away, they wandered to the back of the house. Emma was disappointed by what she saw. A few bushes and trees along the back fence offered some privacy. A tired, old swing set sat in the back corner. *Nobody's used that in a while,* she thought. But she couldn't see any evidence of a garden, nor any kind of a patio or porch. You could tell the house had been vacant for some time. It made Emma feel sad, as she thought about her own yard.

It was a different story, for sure. There you would see twenty-four fruit trees standing in little rows, thriving under Frank Palermo's loving care. Emma's mother and Nona tended a large vegetable garden, where radicchio and arugula flourished. As for the swings, Emma and her sisters loved playing their homemade game of "kick the shoe" on them, singing all the while. This was in addition to the roses, snapdragons, and poppies that grew all summer long in neat little patches around the yard.

Now Emma looked for the statue. She knew a lot of people who had little shrines in their back yards. They usually included statues of Mary, Jesus' mother. Emma saw Anne walk to the back corner, opposite the swings. Emma followed, and when she approached the statue, she frowned. It didn't look like Mary.

"Who is it?" Emma asked.

"It's St. Anne," Anne said.

Now, Emma knew from her religion class that St. Anne was the mother of Mary, but she still had to ask. "Why is she here?"

"'Cause I almost died when I was born, and my mother prayed to her."

Shocked, Emma turned to face Anne. "You almost died? Why?"

"Oh, I didn't get enough oxygen or something like that, and there was a problem with my heart."

"Man, oh, man!" Emma let this news sink in. *No wonder she can't do any running.* "Do you come out here to pray?"

"Not really. Mother used to at the old house." Anne seemed no longer interested in this old topic. She turned and started back toward the house.

Emma took her cue and proceeded to change the subject as she walked beside Anne. "Let's go for a walk," she suggested. "We have a real cool street. I'll show you."

"I have to go tell Mary," Anne responded as she went inside the house. *Why does she act so bored all the time?* Emma wondered as she waited for Anne on the side doorsteps. While Emma waited, a navy blue station wagon pulled up the drive and stopped in front of Emma. Three of Anne's brothers got out. Emma started to panic.

"Hi. Are you waiting for someone?" the oldest boy asked. *OOOOO, please, God, make him go away!* Emma knew she had to be mannerly, but she was too afraid. Still, she tried.

"I'm waiting for Annie. We're going for a walk. I'm Emma from across the street." *That seems to be my new name these days,* she thought as she played with her belt loops.

The boy leaned against the car, cool and content in his khakis and button-down shirt. "Well, I'm David, and this is Tom, and that's Carter," he said, pointing out his brothers. "Larry must be riding." Tom and Carter nodded to Emma as they made their way inside the house. David chose to wait with Emma, and she found herself blushing at the attention. *Man, they really are cute up close. Oh, where is Annie? I don't want to talk to him.* She looked away from David. After all, that's how she treated the boys at school, and it seemed to work there. Only David wasn't to be ignored.

"How long have you lived here?" he asked.

Emma continued to stare at the pavement. "Two and a half years," she managed. *Where is Annie?*

"Do you like it here?" he continued, smiling at her. She knew he was just trying to be nice, but still, she wanted to run away. *Come on, Annie!*

"Oh, I like it just fine," Emma said, and she jumped up when Anne suddenly appeared. "Come on, Annie." Emma couldn't escape fast enough.

"Hi," Anne greeted her brother as she came down the steps.

"Bye, girls. Have fun, and be careful," he said, turning to go inside.

"We will," they answered in unison, strolling down the drive.

Oxford Road looked swell that afternoon, with the sun peeking through the branches of all the glorious trees. Giant lawnmowers buzzed across the Palermos' front lawn, leaving the heavenly scent of freshly cut grass in the air. Robins fluttered here and there, looking for their lunch. Black squirrels chased each other up and down trees. And the stately homes stood in attendance as the girls paraded by.

"This is the Gardners' home over here," Emma said, pointing to her left. "Don't you hate the color of those shutters? Mr. Gardner sells butter and eggs, I think." Emma loved playing tour guide. "And this is the Shelbys' house over here. Mr. Shelby is nice. He just won't let anyone go near his precious tennis court." The girls kept walking down the street. Anne said not a word. "And here is the Lelands' house. They have one daughter, but she's away at camp." Still no comments.

Man, oh, man, it sure is hard to get her to say anything. God, please help me here. Mother said I need to have patience, but I really don't know how, Emma prayed. She was getting discouraged. She loved her street so, and she wanted Anne to like it, too. She sighed and continued her tour.

"This is the home of a man who owns a football team, but I can't remember which one. Their two daughters go away to school, so we won't see them much." There, they had covered the whole block, from the mail box up, but nothing seemed to impress Anne much. They were a few feet from the Palermos' drive, and Emma was losing steam. She stopped and pushed a loose strand of hair behind her ear. She studied Anne's face.

"Would you like to stop now? We can go sit on our patio—would you like that?" Emma offered.

"Okay," Anne blinked. "I don't care."

OOOOOOOOO! Emma screamed to herself. *Why does she have to be like that? I know I have to be nice, but this is too hard.* Emma took a deep breath before she continued. "Okay, come on, then. I'll run upstairs and get my trading cards to show you. I have a nice collection now that Rosalie and Angela gave me theirs." Emma knew she was boasting, but she couldn't help herself.

"What are trading cards?" Anne asked, bursting Emma's bubble.

"You don't know?" Emma was back to square one. *She doesn't know! And she probably doesn't care, either. Oh, man, I don't know about this patience stuff.*

Later that evening as Emma helped her sisters with the dishes, she hoped they could help her. "Hey, guys, how does somebody get patience?" she asked.

"One doesn't 'get' patience," answered Rosalie, rinsing out the glasses. "You have to practice it a while. You just don't go to the store and buy it like ice cream, Emma."

Emma focused her attention on Angela, who was scrubbing a saucepan. "Well, how do you practice it, then?" Angela kept scrubbing. But Rosalie turned to her baby sister and sighed.

"It's like this. Every time you might want to say something nasty or blow off steam at someone, you don't. Like all the times you use my perfume without asking, and I don't yell at you."

Emma thought she understood. "Okay, like today I thought Annie was really silly 'cause she didn't know about trading cards. And I didn't say so."

Rosalie nodded. "Yes, that's it! And what made you resist, by the way? That's not like you." Emma stopped drying and placed the towel on the counter. She didn't like being reminded of her quick temper. "Well," she said, "I said a prayer first."

Angela spun around and flipped her rag in Emma's direction. "That's great! And God heard you. See how all that works?" The two older girls were grinning at Emma now, and that made her feel better. *Maybe I'm on the right track after all,* she thought, pleased with herself.

Rosalie added a note of caution. "You are going to have to practice a lot of patience with Annie. She's not like other girls, you know."

"Yeah, I know," Emma said, scowling. "Mother told me she was special. Man, oh, man, I didn't think it was going to be so hard hanging around her."

Rosalie removed her flowered apron and went to the pantry to hang it up. "But think about this. Annie will probably be a true friend to you if you keep trying," she said.

Emma continued to frown, leaning against the sink. She had never considered her friends "work" before. She thought they were supposed to be fun. Her sisters' suggestions made sense to her, but they also made her uncomfortable. She wasn't sure she liked it.

CHAPTER FIVE

MAKING PROGRESS

The next morning, Emma decided to pursue the subject with her mother. It was time to polish those shoes, and Emma tackled the pile waiting for her on the back stairs. Irene Palermo was around the corner preparing a huge pot of spaghetti sauce, which soon would send its yummy message throughout the house: PASTA TONIGHT!

"Mother, I have another problem," Emma said while she buffed her father's oxfords.

"What is it this time, dear?" her mother asked.

"I never know what to do with Annie. She's so quiet all the time, and she never thinks of things to do. I always feel like I have to entertain her. And I never know if she's happy. She never smiles."

"Well, dear, maybe that's because in the past, she's had no one to really play with. You're lucky, you know. You have sisters. But I bet if you were to sit down and make a list of things you two can do together, you'd come up with quite a few ideas."

"You think so?" Emma was doubtful.

"I know so! And besides, you're turning this into work. Annie doesn't necessarily want to be 'entertained,' as you put it. She just enjoys being with a girl her own age. She likes company like anyone else. Why don't you invite her over for dinner tonight? I bet she likes pasta, and I know your father would like to meet her. But in the meantime, remember to make that list."

"Okay, I'll call her just as soon as I'm done here. I'll ask her to come around five." Emma really liked their plan.

But the doorbell rang at four o'clock. There was Anne, all polished in a fresh sundress, peeking through the glass.

"Oh, man! I told her five o'clock!" wailed Emma as she went to answer the door. "Oh, and she's all dressed up, too!" Emma looked down at her faded Bermuda shorts and frowned.

Rosalie was watching from the piano bench, where she had been practicing, and called after her sister, "Be nice, Emma." But Emma just made a face at her as she yanked open the door.

"Hi. Come in." Emma's tone was anything but inviting.

"Hi," Anne said. She stepped into the foyer and waited. Rosalie knew she had to intervene, so she called out, "Hi, Annie, why don't you come in here and sing with us? Father isn't home yet."

Anne and Emma both looked surprised. Could Anne sing? But Rosalie continued.

"Emma, go get Angela. I think she's reading in her room. Tell her to come and sing. We need her alto."

Without hesitating, Emma headed for Angela's bedroom, hoping her mother wouldn't catch her on the front staircase. *I sure hope Rosalie knows what she's doing!*

The three sisters often sang from their mother's old songbooks while they waited for their father to get home for supper. Their harmony filled the house. And their laughter did, too, for some of the songs were World War I vintage, and the lyrics were comical.

A few minutes later, the three girls surrounded Rosalie at the piano. "Annie, do you have any favorite old songs?" Rosalie asked as she flipped through the sheet music.

"We don't sing much at our house, but David plays the piano."

"That's nice. Let's try this easy one." And with that, Rosalie began the rip-roarin' intro to "Hard Hearted Hannah." The Palermo girls loved to vamp their way through this very peppy tune. The hilarious verses of Hannah's love life always made them smile.

Emma turned to catch Anne's reaction as they both began to sing. *Man, oh, man, she's smiling!* Emma wanted to jump for joy! This would go to the top of her list for sure! Even though Anne's voice fell flat, no one really cared. This was really something to celebrate!

The song ended, and Rosalie found another. And another. Anne didn't know the words or the tunes, but she tried to sing along, anyway. And she smiled the whole time. The music made her feel like a real part of something, and she was having fun!

They ate dinner in the dining room that night, as Anne was considered "company." After Emma's father said grace, all the attention turned to Anne. "Have some pasta. Have more salad. Take some bread."

Why are they fussing over her so? Emma wondered. *She knows how to eat!* Nona Lisa was making such a to-do over Anne that Emma found herself getting a bit jealous. *She's watching her every bite, like some mother bird! This is silly!*

Frank Palermo filled his wine glass and turned to Anne. "We're so happy you could come for supper, Annie. Emma has told us all about you and your family—and your horse, too." Anne looked at him and blinked. And she kept eating her salad.

Emma thought her father looked so rugged and handsome. He had a tan from his construction work, and he looked so cool with his shirt sleeves rolled up and his collar unbuttoned. He tried again to make conversation with their guest. "Are you all settled in over there?" he asked, gesturing with his glass toward the window.

Anne looked at him with her big brown eyes and replied, "All the boxes are gone." And she took another bite of her garlic bread.

"What does your father do for a living?" he went on.

Anne frowned. "I'm not sure. It has to do with insurance, I think." Emma's father smiled and reached for the bread basket. Emma wondered why he was smiling. *Did Annie say something funny?* But then she looked around the table and realized that everyone was smiling. *Man, this is great!* Emma looked down at her plate and smiled as well. Her social life was definitely looking up.

Later, Emma came downstairs in her jammies to say goodnight to her parents. They were in the den. Her mother was reading her *Reader's Digest*. Nona Lisa was dozing next to her on the couch. And Emma's father was trying to read the newspaper in his oversized chair.

Emma came up to him and playfully punched the paper, trying to get his attention. He set the paper down and wrapped his arms around his youngest child, as she settled in his lap.

"Boy, you're getting too big for this," he teased.

Ignoring the comment, Emma started in with her agenda. "What do you think of Annie?"

"Oh, she's quite nice — very mannerly," he said.

"Is that all?" Their noses were inches apart. "Didn't you notice anything else about her?" Emma's mother looked up from her reading and waited for his reply. Emma peered into her father's eyes.

"Oh, she seems pretty quiet. Not at all like someone else I know." Emma's father kissed her nose and tickled her tummy. But Emma resisted. She was trying to be serious.

"You know what I mean! Mother says she's special."

"Well, indeed she is, Emma, but not any more special than my girls. She's just a little different, wouldn't you say?"

"Yeah, I guess so. Mother says I need patience with her." Emma's mother was still listening.

"That is very true—you do. But we all need patience with each other at times." Emma thought for a minute and then tried a different approach.

"Yeah, but she's not like any of my friends at school."

"Well, Emma, that should be a plus for you, don't you think?" Her father always thought so positively. Emma found it irritating at times. One of those times was now.

"Why?" she asked.

"Think about it. You can learn so much more from Annie because she is so different. And her world over there is so unlike ours." Emma wasn't buying what her father was trying to sell.

"But it's hard to be with her sometimes, Father," she admitted in a small voice.

"Ah, she's a challenge for you, then." Father was smiling at her, but she looked away.

"I guess you could call it that."

"You know, Emma, it's up to you to decide whether or not Annie will be your friend. But remember, all good friendships take some effort." Emma remembered Rosalie's words.

"And patience," she added.

"And patience, right!" He hoped his point was getting across.

Slowly, she got up off his lap. She was tired, and she needed more time to think about this. Her father's words were a bit unsettling. They weren't really what she wanted to hear. Leaning over, she pecked him on his cheek. "'Night, Father."

Frank Palermo watched her kiss her mother. His little girl had some growing pains, and he wished he could do more to help her.

"Goodnight, doll," was all he could say.

CHAPTER SIX

LONGING TO BELONG

~~~

Two weeks went by. The Palermo household was full of activity for the Fourth of July weekend. A big family picnic was planned at the Woods Park in honor of Emma's tenth birthday. Emma was so excited, she couldn't sleep.

She could hardly wait to see her cousins, Suzie and Petey-boy, Christine and Dickie. They would play badminton and have three-legged races. They would swim and make sand castles. Emma would watch her mother and two sweet aunts, Bernadette and Virginia, set the yummy food out on the oilcloth-covered tables: Nona's fried chicken, potato salad, and, of course, the buttercream birthday cake! Afterward, they would light sparklers and wait for the fireworks to light up the sky. Mother often called Emma her little firecracker, a title everyone knew Emma deserved.

But now, Emma was helping her mother pack up the food as she sang out with gusto! "I'm as corny as Kansas in August, high as a flag on the fourth of July . . ."

"I'll say you are," her mother interrupted. "Please go get me some more napkins from the pantry, and then I think we're all set."

Angela was out in the garage organizing things in the station wagon. She called out to them, "I'm ready when you are." So far, she had collected the inner tube, three bulging beach bags, the baseball bat, ball, and glove. "Do you think we should take a blanket?" Angela came into the house and was now standing in the kitchen doorway.

"Oh, I think beach towels are enough," Mother answered. "There," she closed the large hamper and gave it a pat. "You ladies may take it away, only be careful."

Emma and Angela grabbed the handles, lifted the basket, and groaned under its weight. "Man, oh, man!" Emma cried. "Are you sure there's food in here and not rocks? This is heavy!" Her mother laughed as she watched the girls proceed down the back hall to the garage.

"Is Annie coming along with us?" Angela asked.

Emma stared at her sister, surprised. "Was I supposed to invite her?"

"Well, you could have. It is your birthday party." They continued toward the open car doors. Then they pushed the picnic basket all the way to the back of the wagon. Emma was thinking.

"Mother didn't say I should invite her. Besides, it's our family picnic."

"Picnics don't have rules, silly. You should have asked her." Angela was busy rearranging the beach bags.

Emma started to feel defensive. "Man, why doesn't anyone ever tell me these things? And do I have to include her in everything I do?" Without waiting for Angela's reply, Emma stomped back into the house, colliding with her mother on the way.

"Ooooooo, Emma, watch where you're going!" Her mother cried as she bent down to retrieve the fallen bags of chips.

"Sorry, Mother." Emma was burning with embarrassment. "Mother, was I supposed to invite Annie today?"

"Well, dear, you certainly could have. She probably would have enjoyed your cousins." Emma's mother continued to the garage with her load.

Emma then remembered something, and her face brightened. She turned back to the garage. "I think that Annie and her whole family were going to their cottage this weekend."

"You can always invite her for next Friday." Mother was inside the station wagon, helping Angela make more space. Emma could hardly hear her. "What's next Friday?"

Mrs. Palermo emerged to answer her daughter. "Why, that's your real family birthday, silly, here at home. Remember, Nona is going to fix you some of your favorites?" Emma smiled.

"Oh, right. Okay, I'll invite her to that! Great!" The problem was solved. She sighed and went in search of the beach ball.

Friday came, and Nona was busy cooking her famous stewed chicken, artichokes, polenta, and gravy. All for Emma! Yum! And the aroma! Double yum!

The dining room table stood like a jewel. Emma had set out her mother's best china, crystal, and silver on the treasured European tablecloth. My, my! All for the birthday girl! Emma stood, surveying the scene. *It's fit for a queen!* She turned in the doorway and waited for Nona to look up from her bubbling pots and pans.

"Nona, what can I do to help with dinner?" she asked. Nona was humming as she stirred away, but she caught sight of her granddaughter, waiting for approval in her new party dress, so she stopped and smiled at her.

"Ah, bella Emma, you look tutta bella!" (which meant "all beautiful"). Nona had a charming way of mixing her English with her Italian.

Emma came to her and gave her a hug. "Thank you for doing all of this for me," she said as she kissed the old woman's worn cheek. "You look nice, too." She pulled away to examine the bubbling pots.

The steam rose to the ceiling, fogging up Nona's glasses. Emma closed her eyes and inhaled.

"How do you like the way I did the dinner table?" Emma asked, fishing for another compliment. Nona chuckled. "Multo lavoro. Too much by hand." Emma understood. All the dishes, silver, and crystal would have to be washed by hand that night. "That's okay. I don't mind doing it." Emma thought that was a small price to pay for such beauty! But she didn't argue.

"What can I do?" she repeated.

Nona thought for a moment while adjusting the pins in her long braids. She walked back to the kitchen table where her game of solitaire was in progress, and then spoke.

"Formaggio. You do?" Again, Emma understood. The Palermos grated their own Parmesan cheese, and Nona needed some to top off the artichokes. Emma opened the refrigerator door and pulled out the chunk of cheese. Next, she found the grater and some waxed paper to set it on.

"And you do aceto, allora?" (*Allora* means "then.") Emma nodded. Their homemade vinegar was kept in a huge keg under the basement stairs. Emma would go and replenish the cruets needed for the salads at the table. But first things first. She began to grate the cheese. And then the doorbell rang. So she went to answer it and this time smiled when she saw Anne's face peering through the glass.

Anne had on another pretty dress, this one lilac, and she held a gaily wrapped present for Emma. "Oh, thank you, Annie," Emma said, taking the gift from her, "I'll open it later, okay? Right now I'm trying to help Nona with a few things in the kitchen. Come on, you can watch."

The girls headed for the kitchen, and when Anne saw Nona at the table, she grinned. *Nona always makes such a fuss over her,* Emma thought as she put the present on the counter with all the others. Tonight was no exception. Nona got up to give Anne a big hug, and Anne laughed. She loved the attention. "Emma, you let Anna do formaggio. You do aceto," Nona instructed. You did not argue with Nona, especially in her kitchen, but Emma would bet that Anne had never handled a cheese grater before in her life! Today, being her birthday, Emma knew that some party manners were called for. So she asked, with the sweetest tone she could manage, "Do you mind helping?"

"I can do this," Anne replied, looking over the utensils on the counter. Emma was doubtful, but she handed Anne the chunk of cheese, grabbed the cruets, and headed for the basement.

Minutes later she returned and checked to see just how much cheese had been grated. "Oh, man," she muttered when she saw the tiny amount. Anne had deserted her job and had taken up her post next to Nona at the stove, sampling the savory tidbits Nona offered from the wooden spoon.

Growing up with Nona in the kitchen, Emma had always been the taste-tester, and now, it seemed, she had been replaced. *I can't be jealous,* Emma thought with a pout, *but I guess I am, a little.* She turned her attention back to the cheese, for she knew her father would be arriving home at any moment.

When the delicious dinner was over and the presents were all opened, Emma's father escorted Anne home. Emma's mother went to the den to catch "I Love Lucy," and Nona stayed to help the girls put the leftovers away. Emma put an apron on and joined her sisters at the sink. They would wash the crystal first. It had been a lovely dinner, but it was over.

"Why you not let Anna wash?" Nona asked Emma. Emma looked up, surprised. "Oh, Nona, she was our guest, and besides, she never washes dishes at her own house."

"No good," Nona said, shaking her head. "He need to help, si!" Nona, like Emma, sometimes confused her pronouns. The granddaughters usually would try to help Nona with this, but not that night. Not when Nona was trying to make a point.

"Why do you say that, Nona?" Emma was confused.

"He need, come si dice, ha bisagna di sentire come appartiene. Capisce?" When something was urgent, Nona's English went right out the window! Emma understood the least amount of Italian in the family, so she turned to her sisters for a translation.

"She's saying that Annie needs to feel like she belongs," Angela offered.

Emma was still puzzled. "How can she do that? By doing the dishes? If she broke any of Mother's good stuff, Mother would have a cow!"

Nona shook her head. "She no break."

Angela and Rosalie sighed, looking at each other. "Emma, you're missing the point," Rosalie said. "It's not about the dishes! It's about being a part of something. Can't you tell? Annie hates to leave here even if it means working alongside us with some silly chore like dishwashing. She doesn't care. Don't you get it?"

It was Emma's turn to sigh now. She was tired, and no, she didn't get it. She didn't want to handle such heavy thoughts on her birthday. "I'm going to bed," she said, and she hugged her Nona. "Thanks for all the great food."

"Okay, okay, buona notte, bella." Nona bid her good night.

CHAPTER SEVEN

WHAT TO DO?

Emma always wondered why they were called the "dog days of August." Dogs, in her estimation, had nothing to do with the fact that she was so tired, so hot, or so bored! She was tired of her books, her records, and her piano. It was too hot to ride a bike or go for a walk or even sit on the patio. Her clothes stuck to her like glue, and her normal "zip" had taken a hike. What to do?

That day, Angela and Rosalie were at their sewing lessons. She was glad she didn't have to go with them. She wasn't the least bit interested in sewing. But how would she spend the afternoon? She dragged herself down the stairs in search of her mother.

Emma found her in the basement. It was made up of several rooms. One had a Ping-Pong table and a blackboard for playing school. The recreation room was handsomely furnished, and it was there that the girls sang and danced on the shiny terrazzo floor. Their mother was in the laundry room folding towels.

"Hi, dear. What are you up to?" Emma's mother asked.

"Nothin' much," Emma muttered, leaning against the doorjamb.

"You miss Annie, don't you?"

Emma thought for a moment. Annie did seem to go everywhere Emma went these days. But the Moreau family had left for their summer home in Canada in early July. Emma felt like Peter Pan, missing his shadow.

"Yeah, I guess so," she said.

"Well, she'll be home soon enough because school starts in a couple of weeks. Can you believe that?" Emma's mother put the clothing down and looked at her sad-sack daughter. "Are you sorry that you didn't go with her for a week like they asked?"

"No . . . I don't know . . . maybe." Emma feared sleeping away from home. No overnights at Nona Palermo's or summer camp for her! Not Emma!

"Maybe I'll go next year," she added, trying to sound brave. "Mother, what will I do about Annie when school does start?"

"What do you mean, what will you do about her?"

"You know, I won't see her much at all." Emma hated to admit it, but this strange little girl, with her strange little ways, had crept into Emma's life and changed it—forever! It was true. Like it or not, Emma was actually learning things from Anne—like patience. Emma was secretly proud of this. But she fretted about the upcoming school term and the changes it would bring.

"What do you mean, you won't see her?" Mother was concentrating on the sheets now. "You'll both get out of school about the same time, so there'll be time before dinner, and, of course, you'll have weekends."

Emma was not convinced. Today it was hard to persuade her of anything. Her mood was so black, she would have scowled at Pat Boone himself! "Man, oh, man, Mother, I'll have my homework to do and my piano, too! How will I be able to help her with her homework?"

"Emma, please, stop now. You do very well in school, and you know it. You won't have that much homework every night. Stop making a mountain out of a mole hill."

Emma moaned. Her mother was always coming up with such corny sayings.

"Besides, we don't even know how much help Annie will need, or even want, from us. There seem to be plenty of helpers at her own house, don't you think?" Emma's mother asked as she arranged the linens in a neat pile.

"Yeah, but if I don't help her with homework, then for sure, I'll never see her."

"Then I guess you have just solved your own problem, haven't you? But relax. We have time to figure these things out. Right now, I need some help with these," and she handed a stack of clothes to Emma. "Here."

The two marched like soldiers all the way up to the bedrooms. After placing her pile on her mother's bed, Emma returned to her own room. The air conditioner didn't work well upstairs, so the rooms were pretty stuffy. But at least she had her privacy, and she wanted to be alone now.

She went to her closet, opened the door, and sat down in front of all the back-to-school finery her mother had just purchased for the new school year. There was the red and blue book bag with the leather straps—so neat! She saw her crisp, plaid school dresses she could wear until Uniform Day. Then she spied her new black-and-white saddle oxfords. How she loved them and the way they smelled. She tried them on, hoping somehow, like magic, they would make all her fears about the days ahead go away. They did look cool, and she did feel so grown up in them. But the misgivings remained, so she reluctantly took them off, got up, and closed the door, sighing. She flung herself on her bed and decided she had no energy to do anything, except maybe take a nap.

CHAPTER EIGHT

A REVELATION

Ten days later, Nona came into the kitchen carrying the mail. "Nina, you see she come?" Emma was busy arranging her trading cards on the big kitchen table and didn't look up. It was almost lunchtime, and Emma knew she had to hurry. "Who's come?" she asked, paying little attention.

"Anna," Nona replied, looking for Emma's reaction. Nothing. So Nona placed the mail on the counter and went to the sink to wash the peaches and plums sitting there.

The news finally registered, and Emma jumped up from her chair. "Really?" She dropped her cards and made a beeline for the front door. It was true! There they were: two big sedans and the station wagon, all parked out front. "Man, oh, man! They're back!" She announced to no one in particular. She had to go find her mother.

"Mother, they're home!" Emma cried as she dashed into the den. Her mother was busy writing a letter and did not look up. "How nice," she said.

"Nona hasn't made lunch yet. Can I call her?" Emma was ready to burst.

"If you mean Annie, no, not yet. Give them a chance to get settled. Go help Nona now with the table. Your sisters are sunbathing on your deck. They don't want lunch. Go on now, scoot."

"OOOOOOO, man!" Emma cried, shaking her hands in protest. *I don't want to set the table!* Emma stomped out of the room and returned to the kitchen. She yanked open the cupboards and pulled out the plates, setting them down hard on the counter.

"Watch those dishes, my dear, or you can buy me some new ones," her mother called. Emma continued to jerk her way around the kitchen, grabbing at utensils and slapping them on the table. Then she flopped herself down on one of the chairs and let out a sigh. "How long do I have to wait?" she whined.

Mother now appeared in the doorway. "You'll have to wait at least until lunch is over."

But the gods were smiling on Emma that day, and she didn't have to wait. The phone rang, and Emma jumped to answer it.

"Hello!" she cried.

"Hi, this is Anne. Can I come over?"

"Sure! Have you had lunch yet? You can eat with us! Nona's making her famous French fries." Emma did a dance around the kitchen with the phone.

"Okay. Bye." And that was that. Emma was grinning from ear to ear as she replaced the receiver. "She's coming over now! That's okay, isn't it?"

Emma's mother smiled as she pulled another dish down from the shelf. "You know, dear, it's very interesting that just a few short weeks ago, you weren't so sure you wanted to be friends with Annie. You thought it would be too much work, remember? And look what's happened. God has rewarded you for being kind."

"And patient," Emma threw in, proud of herself.

"And patient," her mother finished.

Emma started singing, "Hoop di doo, hoop di doo, I hear a polka, and my troubles are through . . ." as she got the milk from the refrigerator. Then she went to get the glasses and almost dropped them when the doorbell rang. "I'll get it!" she squealed and darted from the room.

Emma's mother and Nona looked at each other, grinning and shaking their heads. When Anne entered the room, there were cries of joy and hugs to go around. What a reunion!

"Oh, Annie, welcome home. We missed you!" Emma's mother cried.

"Anna, she so brown," Nona said, noticing Anne's tanned arms. Emma stood there beaming, as if she were personally responsible for all this gaiety. They said grace together and then started on Nona's terrific potatoes, eggs, fruit, and cheese. What a feast!

"Anna, you mangiare di gusto!" Nona said, passing the plate of Asiago cheese. The girls looked to Emma's mother for a translation. "She's commenting on your good appetite, Annie."

Anne smiled, then put her fork down, remembering the reason for her visit. She turned to Emma as she swallowed. "Friday is Mother's birthday, and she wants you to come for dinner."

"Oh, man!" Emma looked so pleased. "I think it's okay." She turned to her mother. "Is it okay, Mother?" *Please don't say no.* Emma was dying to sit in that big formal dining room and eat at that table as long as a football field.

Emma's mother smiled. "Of course you can go. That is so nice of you to ask, Annie. Please thank your mother for us." Emma kept beaming. Her social life was definitely looking up.

Friday afternoon, Emma fussed through her closet for something nice to wear. Summer was almost over, and she was tired of her clothes. She held out her Easter dress for inspection. It wouldn't do with that spot on the front. *How did that get there?* she wondered.

Rosalie appeared in Emma's doorway and seemed to be reading her mind. "Why don't you wear your 'handkerchief' dress? You love that one." The hemline of that dress came to points like those of a handkerchief, and, yes, it was Emma's favorite. She began to search for it. When she found it, way in the back of her closet, she plucked it off of its hanger and looked at it closely.

"You're right. I'll wear this. It looks pretty clean. Too bad I can't fit into anything of yours or Angela's," she said, laying the dress out on the bed.

"Hmf!" Rosalie snorted. "Isn't it bad enough that you take our perfume and our handkerchiefs, and what else?" she teased.

Emma felt hurt. "That's all I take." She went back to the closet for her shoes. Labor Day would be here soon, and her white shoes would have to go. She looked at them closely, as well. They would do.

Rosalie crept over to her little sister's desk to nose around. She picked up the copy of *Photoplay* magazine with Pat Boone on the cover and started to flip through it. She had a favor to ask of Emma, but Rosalie didn't want Emma to think it was too big a deal, so Rosalie tried to appear casual. The favor was really for Angela, but Rosalie was better at getting Emma to do things.

"Are you dining with the whole family tonight?" Rosalie asked Emma, even though she already knew the answer to the question.

"Of course. It's Mrs. Moreau's birthday," Emma said as she searched for her anklet socks.

"Those boys of theirs sure are good-looking. Do you know how old they are?"

"Why, what do you care? You're off to college soon," Emma said. It was true. Rosalie was the first in her family to go to college—Saint Mary's of Notre Dame. She would be leaving in just one week, and the whole Palermo family was as proud as peacocks.

"Well, Angela will be here at home, and I think she would like to know." Rosalie put the magazine down and leaned against the desk.

"Really? You think she wants to know?" Emma asked, buckling her shoe straps.

"Really." Rosalie pretended to examine her manicure. "I'll let you borrow my gold bracelet if you can find out about them."

Now she had Emma's attention. The gold bracelet was a Confirmation gift to Rosalie from Nona Palermo, and Emma had always admired its tiny gold charms and the way they tinkled. *I don't get it, but this must be important,* Emma thought. Now *she* wanted to act casual.

"Really? I can borrow it? That's cool of you. But how about throwing in a squirt of perfume, too? Deal?"

"You got a deal!" Rosalie replied. She smiled as she ruffled Emma's hair. "Let me do your hair for you, too. We want you to look just right."

Emma smiled back. She loved all of this attention. It made her feel as if she were going to the White House instead of just across the street.

"Why are you going to all this trouble for Angela?" Emma asked as her long hair became a beautiful braid.

"Because Angela is a little shy about these things, and she knows you and I talk every now and then. Besides, she's my sister, too, and I want her to be happy."

Emma thought about that for a moment. "I promise to take good care of your bracelet."

"Oh, you just better, my sweet." Rosalie gave the braid a yank. "There, you're all done." And she handed the mirror to Emma.

Emma saw her reflection and smiled. "I'mmmmm ready! Here I come!"

Emma left the house clutching a vase of yellow roses and floated down the drive like a bridesmaid parading to the altar. Since that night was special and since she was "company," Emma decided she would use the Moreaus' front door. Her heart began to pound as she reached for the bell. *Please, God, help me to know what to say,* she prayed, and then she rang.

Hans, looking handsome in his uniform, answered the door. "Hello, Miss Emma, how are you this evening?" he said as he ushered her in.

"Hello, Hans," Emma replied in a tiny voice. *I'm so silly. He doesn't look anything like Vincent Price or Peter Lorre.* She followed him through the entranceway and into the hall. "Wow!" she whispered. The dark, mysterious front hall had somehow come to life, as if Tinker Bell had waved her magic wand. It was all lit up like a Christmas tree! The gilt mirrors gleamed and reflected the glistening chandeliers. *This is just like in the movies!* she thought. And after gazing in wonder for a moment longer, she trailed after Hans.

"Miss Anne, your guest has arrived," Hans said, gesturing toward Emma. He gave Emma a friendly wink and then left. Emma was a bit shaken by all this formality. She didn't know what to think. *Did he just announce my name? Now I know I'm in a movie! Look at them all sitting here so pretty in the drawing room—Colonel Mustard, Mrs. Peacock, and Professor Plum—all waiting to solve that night's big mystery!* Emma smiled at her little joke. *I wish I had remembered to bring my Brownie.* David was to her right, playing the piano. Anne, Carter, and Larry were sitting on the big sofa, looking at photographs, and their parents were down at the far end of the room, enjoying a cocktail by the fireplace. Emma swallowed hard as she stepped into the pretty scene.

"Hello, everybody," she said, smiling at Anne. Emma realized she had to do something with the flowers, so she headed toward Mr. and Mrs. Moreau. Mr. Moreau, in his usual business suit, smiled at Emma as he got up to light his wife's cigarette. Mrs. Moreau sat relaxed and radiant in a silk outfit, the same color aqua as the carpet. Emma watched in awe as he lit the cigarette. *How cool! Father never does stuff like that for mother!* Emma's mother didn't smoke, but Emma was forgetting that.

"Thank you for having me over for dinner," Emma said as she offered the flowers to Anne's mother. "Happy birthday, Mrs. Moreau. These are for you. They're from our garden."

"Why, thank you, Emma. We're so happy to have you. And what a lovely dress you're wearing." Mrs. Moreau leaned over to smell the roses. "Mmmmmm, they're wonderful! Why don't you put them on the coffee table by Anne so we can all enjoy them?" Mrs. Moreau pointed toward her daughter. "Anne, put those away now. Perhaps you can show Emma after dinner." Everyone was smiling at Emma as she placed the flowers near Anne—everyone except David, who was struggling with "Night and Day" on the piano.

"Anne tells us you do quite a bit of singing at your house," Mr. Moreau said. He continued to stand by his wife with his hand on her shoulder. *Man, that is so romantic!* Emma was taking notes. She had to tell her sisters everything!

"Oh, yes, we do," Emma said, truly enjoying the moment. "My sisters are great piano players, and Rosalie is the best sight-reader. My mother gave us some of her old songbooks, so we have a great time. Everyone sings in my family. Even Nona." You could tell that Emma loved this topic. But she would not love where it was headed.

"You know, dear, dinner isn't quite ready yet. Why don't you go over and sing with David? I'm sure he can play something you know," Mrs. Moreau suggested.

Horrified, Emma froze, then swallowed hard, trying to think. She knew Mrs. Moreau was just trying to be nice. *Man, oh, man! I wish Mother were here! Sing with David?*

I can't even talk to David! Oh, oh, oh, who's going to save me? Don't they know I don't sing for strangers? Please, God, help! Emma knew she could not say no. And her smile vanished as she stalled to think of a way out of this dilemma. She looked around the room for an escape and caught sight of Anne. *ANNIE! She can come and help me sing!* Her smile returned.

"Annie, why don't you come and sing, too?" Emma said. *This is funny. Annie is going to help me for a change!*

"Okay." And to everyone's surprise (everyone's except Emma's), Anne got up and marched over to stand next to Emma by the baby grand.

Okay, God, please help us find something simple. We don't want to look too silly, Emma prayed as she watched David flip through his songbook. He gave them a confident smile.

"Well, ladies, what will it be? A little "Tea for Two"?

"Oh, yes!" Emma cried, relieved. "We like that one, don't we, Annie?"

Anne just nodded and grinned. It didn't matter what she sang. She was all for it. She stood there in her pretty eyelet dress, perfectly poised at the piano, as if she had been doing this her whole life. And she waited for the fun to begin.

David found the page and tried out a few chords. "Ready?" Emma nodded. They were ready!

"A one and a two and a three and a four . . ."

"Picture me upon your knee, just tea for two and two for tea . . ."

Anne's voice was monotone, as usual, but Emma's tones were true and strong, carrying the melody throughout the room. She smiled. She could relax and enjoy this. She was in her glory, and Anne was coming along for the ride!

All those in the room stopped what they were doing and stared in amazement. They couldn't believe what they were witnessing. Here was their Anne—who had so much trouble learning anything—singing right along and truly enjoying herself! And there was Emma from across the street, belting out the song like she was born on stage! And it was all happening right there in their living room!

". . . We will raise a family, a boy for you, a girl for me, can't you see how happy we will be!" David ended the song with a flourish. Applause, applause!

Anne whirled around, grinning from ear to ear, and bowed. Everyone clapped and laughed.

Emma was thrilled. She knew something magical had just happened. God had, indeed, answered her prayer, for sure! *Thank You*, she thought as she smiled at the jubilant faces. Mr. and Mrs. Moreau came up to hug their daughter, crying with joy. Hans had entered the room, catching the merriment, and he smiled, too, as he announced, "Dinner is served."

Hours later, the wonderful dinner over, Emma bid good night to all. "I had a great time," she said as she walked to the front door.

"David will walk you across the street, Emma. It's already getting dark out there. Fall is upon us, I'm afraid," Mr. Moreau said, checking his watch.

Emma could smile at David now. He had joked with her at dinner, so she was no longer afraid of him. He was a high school senior and really knew how to talk to people.

"See you soon, Annie," she said as she followed David outside.

"You've got quite a pair of lungs, there, kiddo," David said, strolling down the drive.

Emma was glad he couldn't see her blush in the fading light. "Everyone in my family does," she said. "We sing all the time—while doing dishes, in the car, on the swings playing . . ."

"Playing what?"

"Oh, just a little game we invented." Emma caught herself. She couldn't tell an outsider about "kick the shoe"!

"Oh, yeah? Sounds like fun. Speaking of fun, thanks for being so nice to my sister."

"That's okay. My mother always says, 'The more the merrier.'"

They came to Emma's front step and stopped. "Well, here you are. Guess I'll see you at Thanksgiving," David said.

This took Emma by surprise. It also reminded her of her deal with Rosalie. "Why Thanksgiving?" she asked. "Where are you going?"

"Tom and I have to leave for school next week. It's my last year, and Tom will be a sophomore."

"Where's school? Far?" she asked, hoping for more information.

"Massachusetts," he replied.

"Massachusetts? Man! That's far!" Emma had no clue how to say good night to a boy, so she did the only thing she could think of—she stuck out her hand for him to shake. "Have a good trip," she added. He shook her hand and turned to leave. Emma went inside.

There she found Angela waiting for her on the stairs in the dark. "Hi," Emma whispered. "Hi. Did you have a nice time?" Angela whispered back. *Oh, man,* thought Emma, *Angela isn't going to like what I have to tell her.* "It was just like in the movies. Let me go say good night to Mother and Father, and I'll tell you all about it upstairs."

A few minutes later, Emma, now in her jammies, began to tell what happened at dinner. Angela sat on the edge of the bed, waiting. "Just tell me about the boys," Angela pleaded. Emma knew what she meant. But she sure hated being the bearer of bad news. She sat down on the opposite bed and looked her sister in the eye.

"Well," Emma paused, struggling for the easiest way to say this, "David is a senior, and Tom is a sophomore, and they go to school . . ."

"Where?" Angela urged her.

Emma squeezed her eyes shut as she answered, "In Massachusetts."

"Where?" Angela didn't think she had heard right.

"In Massachusetts. And they leave next week, too." Did she dare open her eyes now?

"Before Labor Day?" Angela couldn't hide the disappointment in her voice.

"I guess so." Emma sighed and looked at Angela's sad face. She felt terrible for her sister, but she was way too tired to continue. She hadn't even brushed her teeth yet, but she didn't care. All she wanted to do was plop herself right into bed.

"That's awful," Angela cried as she got off the bed to leave.

"David doesn't play the piano half as well as you." Emma thought a compliment might ease the pain somehow.

"Thanks," Angela said wistfully. "Well, good night, I guess." She turned and left.

"Good night to you, too." Emma yawned and rolled over on her bed to grab the pillow. She thought about Anne and how surprised everyone was when she started singing! Emma smiled. *I can't imagine a house without singing! That's almost sacrilegious! Glad I don't live there,* she thought. "Thank You, God, for everything tonight. Please help Angela feel better." In her dreams, she danced with Vincent Price while Anne danced with her father. Mrs. Moreau danced with Hans, the butler, while all the boys looked on, smiling.

CHAPTER NINE

A MOUNTAIN AND A MOLE HILL

School began, and Emma soon immersed herself in a world of uniforms, early bedtimes, new textbooks, and old friends. She belonged to room #210, a split class of fifth- and sixth-graders. Emma had never been part of a split class before, but she knew things would go well with Sr. Marie Anne, who was in charge. Kerry O'Toole, Emma's secret crush, was in her class, along with the twins, Beth and Laura Ames. Everyone looked wonderful, she thought, just a little bit taller. And she hoped that this year, she would get up the nerve to speak to Kerry. After all, she had practiced with David, hadn't she? The new school year held much promise for her, and by the end of the first week, Emma was already in sync with her new routine . . . minus Anne, of course.

When Friday afternoon arrived, Emma found herself with a bit of homework. So she put on her shorts and hauled her books out to the patio, as the weather was still warm. She wanted to get the reading for her book report out of the way so she could enjoy her weekend. As she settled in a lounge chair, she heard the phone ring. She chose to ignore it. But Mrs. Palermo opened the screen door and called to her. "Emma, it's for you. It's Annie."

"Oh, man," Emma cried. *How am I supposed to juggle all of this and Annie, too?* She just couldn't see how this would work. But she closed her reader and headed inside. Her mother was watching as Emma picked up the receiver.

"Hello," Emma said.

"Hello, this is Anne."

"Hi, Annie." Emma refused to say more.

"I'm having trouble."

Uh oh, here it comes, Emma thought. "Trouble with what?" She pretended not to know.

"My arithmetic. Can you help me?" Anne asked.

Emma looked at her mother, who stood there, waiting and listening. Emma knew very well what her mother would have her do. But Emma was tired and wasn't feeling very generous at the moment. She sighed. *I don't think I have a choice.*

"Yes, I can help. I'll be over in a little bit." Emma wasn't used to putting the needs of her friends before her own. She began to feel a little rebellious. *Man, it's just not fair!* She looked at her mother with tears in her eyes as she hung up the phone.

"How am I supposed to do two sets of homework and then my piano and still have time for fun? I told you this would happen, Mother. I can't be in two places at once," Emma cried.

"Dear, don't go exaggerating now. Just go over there and see exactly what she needs help with." Emma's mother moved away from Emma and started to set the table for dinner. "You won't be doing this every night. You can explain this to Annie in a nice way when you see her." As Mrs. Palermo paused to gather some napkins from the drawer, she looked at her daughter and saw two big fat tears rolling down Emma's cheeks. Mrs. Palermo put the napkins down and went to give

Emma a hug. She pressed Emma's head to her heart. Emma just stood there angry and helpless.

"Oh, honey, helping Annie shouldn't be such a terrible burden for you! There is a way to work this all out. We just haven't found it yet. You'll see. You've had a busy week and a lot going on. And I know you're probably tired. Things will calm down. You wait."

Emma wiped her eyes with her sleeve. She was too miserable to talk about this anymore. So she wiggled out of her mother's embrace and headed for her bedroom. And on the way, she turned her head toward the den and noticed Nona there. Nona motioned for her to come in. *She must have overheard us,* thought Emma. With a heavy heart, she went and sat next to her Nona on the couch.

Nona was in the middle of her rosary, those beloved brown wooden beads. She sat there so peacefully in her faded housedress. She looked Emma in the eyes and raised the hand fingering the beads. "Try," she said. "She help."

Emma smiled. She so admired her Nona's deep and quiet faith. She hoped that it would rub off on her someday. She leaned over and pecked Nona's cheek, then left the room. She had to wash her face. Though she didn't have time for a whole rosary, she did say a prayer while combing her hair. "Dear God, I need more patience. Please send me lots. I have work to do here, and Annie needs me over there, and I don't know how to be in two places at once. Please help me."

Emma left her house without a word. Instead of going directly to Anne's, Emma made her way down to the lake. It was calm and very blue that day. She sat on the little bench of the slate-roofed bus stop and watched the cars go by. Emma let out a big sigh, thinking she was alone. Then she heard a familiar voice.

"Is that our dear Emma from across the street?" It was Mary, appearing out of nowhere, like an angel!

"Hello, Mary," Emma said and tried to smile.

"Now, what would a fine young person such as yourself be doing waiting for a bus at this hour?" Mary joked.

Emma's face brightened. "Oh, I was just taking a walk—on my way, actually, to help Annie with her homework. Do you know if she's got a lot?" Emma scrunched up her face, as if in pain.

Mary dropped the letters she had been holding into the nearby mailbox. "Well, the thing about Anne and her homework is that it never really seems to get done."

Emma's eyes were wide open now. "Never?" she asked in disbelief.

"But that's not for you to trouble yourself with," Mary said as she stood waiting for Emma to stand and join her.

"The truth is, I don't have much practice tutoring people," Emma said, frowning, as she rose from the bench.

"That shouldn't be a problem, dearie. Hans and Madelaine and myself—we are not tutors, either, but we all give it a try when there's a need and we have some time."

Emma felt a wave of encouragement come over her. Mary was the answer to her prayer!

"Just do what you can for the moment, Emma. That is all anyone can ask, and Anne will be so happy. You'll see," Mary said, linking her arm with Emma's. Emma beamed with relief. And the two turned from the lake and the traffic and strolled back up Oxford Road.

An hour later, Emma walked back through her front door. Rosalie was pounding "Rustles of Spring" on the piano, and Nona was cooking something swell! These comforting things reassured Emma that there was an order to her life and that things with Anne would fall into place. Emma thought about this as she waltzed into the kitchen to check the time on the Philco clock radio. *Hmm,, 4:30—almost time for dinner.*

There in the kitchen, Angela was busy making the salads and measuring out the dressing—lots of vinegar for her father and Emma, a wee bit for everyone else. "Are you finished helping Annie already?" Angela asked.

Bet she was talking to Mother, Emma thought. "Yes, I am—for today, anyway."

"How did she do?"

"Not real well. She can read and write, some. Her spelling is bad, and her handwriting is terrible, but she's really stumped with her arithmetic." Emma watched with fascination as Angela cut up the radishes.

"Are you going to go back?" Angela asked.

"Maybe. Next week. Man, their house sure feels like a tomb with David and Tom gone."

"Oh, where were Carter and Larry?"

"Larry was out riding, and Carter was doing his own homework, I guess."

"Does Mrs. Moreau know you are helping Annie?" Angela continued to be nosey.

"Oh, I don't know. She wasn't around, but it doesn't matter. I don't see how much difference I can make."

Nona came into the room to check on her pot of risotto. "Potete fare buon mostrandoglieli cura, provando," she said.

Emma waited for a translation from Angela.

"She's telling you that the good lies in your going over to help, not in how many arithmetic problems you solve." Angela kept cutting, Nona kept stirring, and Emma stood there, thinking.

"Mary said practically the same thing to me today."

Angela looked up with a look that said, "See?" Emma moved to the stove to give her Nona a hug. "Why are you so smart?" Emma said.

"'Cause I go to school forever, bella." They all laughed, knowing that Nona, with only three years of education, still possessed the wisdom of the ages. And they loved her for it.

CHAPTER TEN

FACING HER FEARS

The weeks flew by, and Oxford Road took on the red and gold colors of fall. Rosalie departed for Saint Mary's, and Angela immersed herself in Patrick Henry's speeches. Soon, everyone would know the line "Give me liberty, or give me death!" Emma's mother got busy changing closets, clothing, and bedding. And Emma went back and forth to Anne's, helping with homework. But with each week, Emma's frustration grew.

"Mother, things are just getting ridiculous over there," Emma complained one Thursday afternoon. She had just returned from the Moreaus' and went stomping into the den to find her mother. Mrs. Palermo was darning socks and trying to catch some news on TV when Emma planted herself right in her mother's way, crossing her arms and looking disgusted. Emma's mother looked up from her needlework and tried not to smile.

"Why are things so ridiculous, dear?"

"Because they are."

"Well, you'll have to be more specific, Emma, if you want me to understand."

"Because we're not getting anywhere." Emma flopped herself down on the couch next to her mother.

"Be careful, there, girl; you'll get stuck with one of my needles," her mother warned.

Emma took a quick look at the couch cushions and then turned to her mother, almost pleading, "Mother, must I keep going over there?" It was clear Emma wanted to bail out of her homework sessions with Anne.

"How does Annie feel about the work you do?" Emma's mother asked.

Mother isn't going to make this easy. "She seems okay with it. She puts the papers we do in this green folder and takes them to the nuns the next day. But it's never very much."

Emma's mother stopped her mending and looked Emma in the eye. "Emma, you're judging the amount of work you do by whose standards? Yours, I'm afraid. Didn't I tell you that you and Annie are like apples and oranges, not apples and apples?"

"I know," Emma pouted, punching a throw pillow.

"If Annie has a page or two to show the sisters, I'm sure she thinks that's grand. And it is, for her." Emma's mother turned back to her work. "Is anyone telling you a different story?"

Emma sat still and just frowned at the pillow. "No, but I feel like I'm moving in slow motion when I'm helping her."

"I'm hearing the word 'I' a lot here," her mother said. "And you *are* moving in slow motion with Annie, I'm afraid. But you have to remember, this is not about you. This big favor you're doing is about Annie. And you won't be helping her along at all if you insist on moving at your speed. This will all turn into one big nightmare!"

Emma was silent. *Why does Mother always have to be right? She's not going to let me off the hook. Not today, anyway.* "I suppose you're right," Emma sighed.

"Suppose so? I know so! Now, tell me about your own homework. How is it coming along?"

Emma got up to leave. "I have spelling to finish."

Mrs. Palermo looked up at her child, "You're doing a great thing here, Emma. There's no denying that. I just hope you won't give up the ship—not yet, anyway. Real friends don't do that." How could Emma say no? She didn't want to make her own mother beg.

The next day was Friday and the end of the week. Emma sang as she changed from her school uniform into her pedal pushers and loafers. She was so happy to have the weekend! With only three pages of Chopin to practice, she would soon be free, free, free! But as she skipped toward the living room, something made her stop dead in her tracks.

At the front door, ready to ring the bell, stood Mrs. Moreau! She had never visited the Palermo home before. Oh, the Moreaus and the Palermos had chit-chatted outside of church on several occasions, but never at each other's homes. And now here was Mrs. Moreau! She looked lovely, too, in an elegant pair of navy slacks and a matching sweater. *She would look great in a potato sack,* Emma thought. *What is she doing here? Did Mother invite her?* Emma went to open the door. "Hello, Mrs. Moreau. Come in."

"Hello, Emma. I hope I'm not intruding. Is your mother free a minute?" Michelle Moreau stepped into the foyer, looked around, and smiled. "This will only take a moment. What a lovely home you have."

Emma stood there like a statue. *This is so weird! Annie's mother in our house!* But then she remembered her manners. "Thank you. Why don't you come in here and wait while I go and find Mother?" Emma gestured toward the living room. She looked at it quickly. This room was always neat. No one ever came in here unless they were playing the piano. She showed Anne's mother to a seat on the big brocade couch. But it was the fireplace mantle that caught everyone's eye when they entered the room, and Michelle Moreau walked over to it and touched the shiny, white marble.

Emma left her there and darted up the forbidden staircase in search of her mother. *Where is she?* Emma peeked in all the bedrooms and finally found her in the guest room.

"Mother!" Emma gasped. "Mrs. Moreau is down in the living room. She wants to speak with you."

"Oh, how nice. Just let me put these towels away, and I'll be right behind you." Mrs. Palermo looked up from her piles. Emma was standing there. "Go on, now, scoot! See if she would like something to drink."

Emma continued to stare at her mother, who was wearing one of her plain housedresses. "Aren't you going to change?" Emma asked.

Her mother kept arranging the folded towels. "Change? Of course not. Don't be silly! Now go. I'll be right there."

Emma found Mrs. Moreau settled in a chair by the fireplace, smoking a cigarette. "Mother will be right down. Would you like some lemonade?"

"Oh, no, Emma. Thank you. I just came over to ask you something and to see if your mother would approve."

Emma was really curious now. She sat very still on the couch with her hands folded in her lap, staring at the smoke as it made its way to the ceiling. *Wonder what it's like to smoke? What does she want to ask Mother?* she thought. The suspense was killing her.

Emma's mother finally joined them. "Oh, hello, Michelle. It's so nice to see you," Emma's mother said in her most gracious tone.

Emma couldn't help but notice the difference between the two ladies—Mrs. Moreau, sophisticated in her silk slacks, smoking a cigarette; and her own, dear, wonderful mother in her not-so-wonderful housedress!

"I hope I'm not interrupting, Irene. I just wanted to come over and thank Emma for what she's doing for Anne."

Emma's eyes popped. *She knows about the homework! Please, God, don't let her be mad!* Emma looked down at her hands as her mother responded.

"Oh, that's nothing. Emma's so happy to be of help. Aren't you, dear?" she said, giving Emma an "I told you so" look.

Emma managed a feeble smile. "Sure," she said, feeling so ashamed.

"I just wanted to thank Emma, so I thought perhaps she'd like to come and stay overnight at our house tomorrow. Dad is going to take Anne to see the Pat Boone movie *April Love*. It's at the Woods theater."

Emma froze. She didn't know what to say! Overnights—anywhere—horrified her, but she really wanted to see that movie! She looked at her mother for help.

"Oh, I think Emma would love that, wouldn't you, dear?" Emma's mother sent an encouraging smile in her daughter's direction.

"Sounds nice," Emma managed, her feelings of panic rising. But Mrs. Moreau just went on, not noticing.

"I know I could have phoned, but I really wanted to thank you in person for spending so much time with Anne and her homework. Anne seems so much happier going to school these days." Emma just nodded in agreement.

Mrs. Moreau put out her cigarette and stood up. "We'll have dinner at six because the show starts at 7:30. Dad will be so thrilled to have two beautiful dates!" Emma's mother walked her to the door, and Emma trailed.

"This is so nice of you, Michelle," Emma's mother said.

"Oh, no! The pleasure is all ours. We're so lucky to have your wonderful family right across the street!" She turned to Emma. "Can you come around 5:30?"

"Okay. Thank you," Emma said, feeling like she wanted to throw up.

Mother opened the door. "Well, thanks again for the invitation. Give our best to Louis."

"Oh, I will. You have a great evening." She went down the steps and down the drive.

Once the door was closed, Emma exploded. "Oh, Mother, what am I going to do? I never even stay overnight at Nona Palermo's like Rosalie and Angela do! How can I do this?"

Emma's mother put her arm around Emma's shoulders and walked her to the kitchen. "Don't you think it's about time, my dear, that you got over this?" Her mother was using her gentlest voice.

"Oh, I knew this homework thing with Annie would get me into trouble." Emma felt trapped.

"Trouble? What trouble? You're going to a movie, and then you're going to spend the night right across the street. Where is the trouble?"

Emma scowled and folded her arms in anger. Her emotions were all jumbled. She wanted to help Anne, but she didn't. She wanted to see this movie in the worst way, but she didn't want to stay overnight at Anne's house. Why did everything have to be so complicated? Why couldn't things be the way they used to be before she ever met Anne?

"You know, everyone over there loves you, even the servants! It's not like they're a bunch of strangers, for heaven's sake. Your social life is calling you, Emma. How about it?"

Emma continued to grouse in the kitchen doorway. "My social life shouldn't feel so much like work! It should all be fun!"

"And it will be, if you just let it," her mother added as she went to the pantry for some aprons. "Please come in here now and cut up these tomatoes for me. I need them for the pepperonata. They're over there on the windowsill. You can practice your piano later."

Emma took the apron and put it on. "What if I get scared in the middle of the night? Or sleepwalk?"

Her mother laughed, "Ha, ha! You haven't walked in your sleep in years! I doubt that will happen. No, once you get there, you'll be fine. You'll see." Her mother tried to be reassuring.

Emma slashed away at the tomatoes, wishing she could feel half as confident as her mother.

Though dinner the following evening was not quite as formal as the birthday party, things were still pretty different from the way the Palermo family dined. At the Moreaus', no one passed dishes of food, family-style. Hans came and served everyone individually. If you wanted more of something, Mrs. Moreau pressed a hidden button, and PRESTO! Hans appeared to deliver it! The long table seemed empty with Tom and David gone. And though the chandeliers were lit, the room had a somber air. Only Carter's and Larry's occasional joking around gave the room some life. *Thank goodness for their giggling. It's too quiet in here,* Emma thought. But she would soon regret that.

"Do you go to the movies often, Emma?" Mr. Moreau asked, buttering his roll.

Emma had to chew her bite of salad fast so she could answer him. "Once in a while. I go with my cousin, Christine, or my sisters to the Sunday matinees. *Am I using the right fork?* she wondered.

"And what kind of movies do you like?" he asked.

"Oh, we usually go see John Wayne or some other Western." Emma heard some giggles and wondered if they were aimed at her. *What's wrong with Westerns? I love watching "Cheyenne" on TV. And someone please tell me what these little green things are!* Emma stared at the capers on her plate. Not wanting to take a chance, she turned her attention to her potatoes.

"Do you want to go to Saint Mary's, too, when you get older?" Mrs. Moreau asked, trying to change the subject.

"Oh, maybe. It's a pretty small school. I think Angela wants to go next year."

"And what would you like to study when you go to college?"

"Father thinks I'd make a good architect. We go over his blueprints all the time together." Emma was pleased to talk about her dreams.

More giggles. Emma looked around, frowning. Then she continued, "Or I might become a nun."

The boys let out a roar of laughter! Emma put her fork down. She could feel her face getting red as she looked around the table, trying to figure out just what was so funny.

"Boys! That will be enough!" Mr. Moreau commanded. There was silence.

"Oh, Emma, I do apologize for the boys' rudeness. They are in such a silly mood tonight. But you have no idea how cute you are." Mrs. Moreau gave Emma one of her glorious smiles.

Emma was close to tears, but she refused to cry in front of Anne's family. *I'm not trying to be cute! Why would they think that? I'll have to ask Annie about this later. Cute, my eye!* She picked up her fork and finished her meal. Dessert couldn't come soon enough.

The movie, of course, was grand. Pat Boone was so handsome, and the music was so lovely. Emma tried to memorize it right there on the spot. She hummed as they all came into the house. She hummed as the girls made their way up the grand staircase, but then she stopped. They had reached Anne's bedroom. *Oh God, please don't leave me now! Please help me,* she prayed.

To Emma's surprise, Mary entered the room to turn down the beds. She also helped Anne change her clothes and arrange her toothbrush. Emma was amazed! No one ever fixed her bed or her Pepsodent—not since she was a very little girl.

When they were in their pajamas, they piled into the twin beds. They were so comfy, and the covers were so cozy! Emma hadn't realized 'til now how tired she was. She stretched out and turned her head to see if Anne was going to say her prayers. But Anne just smiled. Mary, who was waiting for them to get settled, tried to reassure Emma.

"Why don't I just leave the light in the bathroom on for you dears so you can see your way if you need to?"

Emma let out a big sigh of relief. *Mary is such an angel!* "Oh, thank you, Mary. That would be great! Good night."

"Good night, girls. Don't let the bed bugs bite." And Mary left them.

Anne yawned. Emma smiled and looked around. In the semi-darkness, the room wasn't half as scary as she had imagined it would be. *Mother was right. Thank You, God, for helping me.*

CHAPTER ELEVEN

MORE PROGRESS

The days before Thanksgiving were cold and crisp. Oxford Road took on a skeletal appearance as the leaves from all the elms continued to fall. Normally, Frank Palermo had help from Mr. Ottway with the lawn, but raking the leaves was a tradition reserved for the Palermo girls. Their father would push the piles of leaves into the street by the curb and burn them. What could beat the smell of burning leaves in the fall? With Rosalie gone, they were one helper short, but Emma didn't mind. She knew her big sister would be home soon with all kinds of stories to tell. Emma could hardly wait. She hummed as she raked, thinking about the days ahead.

The cold air made Emma's nose run. When she stopped to wipe it, she saw Anne walking across the street. Anne shoved her hands into her pockets as she came over to investigate. No one burned leaves at her house. They were simply hauled away.

Emma smiled at Anne. If you didn't know better, you would think that Anne had just stepped out of a lumber camp with her plaid jacket and blue jeans. *Blue jeans! How did she get out of the house with those on?* Emma wondered. Mrs. Moreau did not approve of jeans.

"Hi," Emma called, still sniffling. Her nose was so cold! But it was starting to get dark, so she kept raking.

"Hi," Anne said, standing by Emma, watching her rake.

Frank Palermo looked up and called to them, "Be careful with the piles, Annie," as he gestured toward the smoking leaves. Anne nodded and waved.

"What's going on?" Emma asked, pausing to wipe her nose again.

"Nothing much. Can I rake, too?"

Emma looked at the Moreau house. She thought of Nona's words about including Anne in whatever Emma was doing, but she didn't think Mr. and Mrs. Moreau wanted their daughter raking leaves. "We're almost done. It's getting late, and I was just about to go in the house."

"Well, can we play cards later?" Anne asked.

Emma grinned. It seems she had created a monster of sorts. Since Emma had taught Anne to play rummy two weeks before, it was all Anne wanted to do! Anne knew how to play old maid, so Emma thought she would try to teach Anne rummy. And wonder of wonders, Anne had caught on. After many attempts, she could play the game. Emma knew Anne wanted to practice so she could impress her brothers when they came home for the holiday.

"Not tonight, Annie. I have two tests tomorrow. Maybe this weekend. I promise. When do your brothers get home?"

"Mother said ten days."

"Oh, so soon? Well, we still have time to practice up. Don't worry. You'll beat 'em." Emma shoved her Kleenex back into her pocket and then took off her gloves.

Emma's father came over to haul her pile into the street. It was the last one. "Thanks, sweetie," he said. "You girls better go in now. It's getting dark. Tell Mother I'll be in soon. Are you staying for supper, Annie?"

Anne stood there looking at Emma. *Whenever she can,* thought Emma. And she smiled at Anne as the two walked into the house.

The ten days flew by. While Emma was setting the table in the dining room, she peeked through the drapes and couldn't help but notice that every single light at the Moreau house was on—a sure sign that David and Tom had come home.

"The boys are home," Emma announced to anyone within earshot.

"How do you know?" her mother asked from the kitchen.

"Their bedroom lights are on, as well as every other light in the house!"

"Oh, Emma, please don't go staring out those windows!" her mother scolded.

Emma returned to her task, humming as she went. The boys' arrival meant that Rosalie soon would be home as well. And the holidays would be here, and oh, what fun they would all have! She went into the kitchen for more silverware and saw her mother cleaning mushrooms at the sink.

"Nona is making fungi tonight. Uncle Louie picked them in the fields while he was hunting last week," her mother said, gathering the mushrooms in the colander.

"Oh, man, Mother; did he shoot anything?" Emma was intrigued with the men in her family who went hunting, especially her sweet Uncle Louie. She just couldn't picture him carrying a gun and chasing after deer and rabbits.

"No deer this time, but he got three pheasants. We'll cook those next week when Rosalie's here."

"Oh, Mother, I just can't wait for her to get here," Emma groaned as she searched for more spoons.

"I know, dear. We're all anxious to see her."

"Do you think she'll be different?" Emma looked concerned and stopped to catch the look on her mother's face.

"Why do you think that?" her mother answered, trying to keep the worry out of her voice.

"Oh, I don't know. She's a big college girl now." Emma went back to the dining room.

"Well, she's still your sister," Emma's mother called after her, hoping this made sense.

The day finally arrived. It was the Tuesday before Thanksgiving, and Emma was so excited, she felt like jumping out of her skin! "Oh, please, Mother; please let me go with Father to pick her up!" "Her" meant Rosalie, and she was arriving soon at Michigan Central Train Station.

The house was in a state of confusion. Angela had put on her brand new baby blue slacks, and Mother wore a new dress underneath her apron. They were helping Nona prepare a special "welcome home" dinner for Rosalie. There was much banging of the pots and pans as they proceeded with the pasta and the pole beans—the last of the season from Nona's garden. But Emma didn't want to get caught up with cooking or kitchen duties that night. She just wanted to fly out the door the minute her father showed his face.

"Yes, yes, you may go and keep Father company. I'll stay here and try to keep Angela from breaking too many dishes," her mother joked.

"Mother!" Angela protested. "I'm not breaking any dishes. I'm just trying to find the lid to the saucepan."

"It's right there, dear, under that towel. It's hiding on you." With that, everyone laughed, relieving some of the tension.

"What's so funny in here?" asked Emma's father as he came in the side door, smiling at the sight of his busy ladies.

"FATHER!" Emma shrieked, rushing to him. "I get to go with you to get Rosalie!" And she threw her arms around his neck to kiss him. Her father shot a quick glance at her mother, but her face said, "It's okay."

"Well, let me come in and say hello before we say goodbye." He laid his briefcase on the counter. Mother came over to kiss him, and Angela was right behind her. Nona just stood by the sink, arms folded, nodding and smiling.

"Looks like we have plenty of cooks tonight, Emma, so yes, you get to ride along with me. I just want to go and change my shirt and wash my hands, okay?" And her father headed for the stairs.

Emma sang all the way to the train station, "There's a big fat turkey down on Grandpa's farm, and he struts around all day. . . ." She could not contain her excitement. And when she saw Michigan Central, her eyes bugged out. The size and grandeur of the station overwhelmed her. Such fancy ceilings! And so high! So many people going in so many directions! She held her father's hand and gazed all around, trying to locate the voice announcing the arrivals and departures. The big filigree gold clock drew everyone's attention, and Emma's eyes were bright with admiration. "Oh, Father, this is just like in the movies!" she exclaimed.

"We're over here." Her father pointed to his left, and they walked across the huge expanse.

Emma was fascinated by all the activity: the man selling magazines, the one selling hot dogs, and even the one shining shoes. "I can't wait to tell Mother!"

"Take good notes, dear. Your mother has never been here, either." Emma looked up at her father, feeling guilty. *Mother could have come down here to get Rosalie instead. She let me come in her place,* she thought.

"I'm sure your mother wanted you to see all of this," Emma's father said, reading her thoughts. "Emma, help me find track #27 now." Together they started searching the rows and rows of tracks for the right one. Her father looked at his wristwatch.

"Are we on time?" Emma asked, a little anxious.

"Oh, yes. In fact, we're a few minutes early. The train should come right along here, and very soon."

Emma had worn her Sunday coat and hat and even her gloves so she would look just right for Rosalie. But the waiting was killing her, and she proceeded to hop from one foot to the other to keep warm and to shake away her nervousness. A few minutes passed, and then they heard the whistle!

"Ooooh, that's loud!" Emma cried. She closed her eyes and blocked her ears.

"That's because the train is so close, and it's coming right inside this building!" her father shouted back. He pointed to the approaching train. "Look, Emma, it's here!"

The massive engine appeared amidst a veil of steam, creeping toward them and then coming to a complete stop just twenty feet away.

"It's here! It's here! Where's Rosalie?" Emma cried. The wait was over, but she still couldn't spot her sister. She stared at everyone getting off the train, and then she smiled.

Rosalie came down the steps onto the platform and turned to look. Standing there in her beautiful new Polo coat and her velvet beret, she waved at her father and Emma. Her father rushed up to greet her, then took her suitcase. Emma ran after him.

"Rosalie! Rosalie! You're home!" Emma cried, throwing herself into her sister's arms. Emma could smell the familiar perfume as she buried her face in her sister's scarf. She looked up into Rosalie's face. *Oh, she looks different! What is it, the hat?* Emma thought as tears sprang to her eyes.

"Hello, little sister. Did you think I wasn't going to make it?" Rosalie kissed Emma's forehead.

"I missed you so much!" Emma blubbered.

"Well, I missed you, too. Come on, let's go home now. I missed everybody!" Their father was beaming as he took

Rosalie's arm. Emma grabbed Rosalie's free hand, and together they left the station for Oxford Road.

When the "welcome home" dinner was over, Emma sat on Rosalie's bed and watched her unpack. "You look different," Emma noted.

"Oh, why do you say that?"

"I don't know. You look a little older."

"Well, silly, I am a bit older." Rosalie straightened up from her dresser drawers and stared at Emma. "You—you are the one who's changed! I bet you've grown at least two inches since Labor Day!" Emma just grinned. She wanted to know what Saint Mary's was like, so she just came out with it.

"Do you have any boyfriends at school yet?"

Rosalie plopped down on the bed and hugged her. "No, miss nosey, and if I did, I wouldn't be telling you!"

"Oh, poop!" Emma said, disappointed.

Rosalie thought to change the subject. "How are things going with Annie these days?"

"Oh, I go over there and help her with her homework, and she comes here a lot, too, when she's not riding. I taught her to play rummy."

"Really? I didn't know you liked to play cards."

"I don't. But someone had to take your place playing gin with Father—so I taught myself, and then I taught Annie." Emma was proud of this, too.

"Well, that is really neat!" Rosalie was amazed. "What a grown-up thing to do! What else has been going on around here that I should know about?"

"Oh, not much. Angela won another speech contest. Uncle Louie caught three pheasants; Nona's going to cook them on Saturday. And I went to the movies and stayed overnight at Annie's." She tried to sound casual as she mentioned this last bit of information.

But the comment wasn't lost on Rosalie. She jumped off the bed and stared at her sister.

"You stayed overnight? At someone's house? You? Really?" She was flabbergasted.

Blushing, Emma got up from the bed and straightened the spread. "Yes, we saw Pat Boone in *April Love*."

"But Emma! You stayed overnight! Away from home!" Rosalie couldn't get over it.

"Yes, I did," *I wish she'd stop gushing about it,* she thought.

"That is so great! You are the one who's changed, not me!"

Emma was getting embarrassed, so she headed for the bedroom door. "I have to change for bed now." And she left with Rosalie still standing there with her mouth open.

CHAPTER TWELVE

MORE CHALLENGES

The day before Thanksgiving, the sisters went shopping. After a little begging, the girls borrowed their father's brand new Ford Thunderbird—a snazzy bronze sports car. Even though it was a two-seater, the girls didn't care. They were so happy to be together again and to be starting a holiday that the size of the car didn't matter at all. They joyfully squeezed in and planned their route. They would stop at all their favorite haunts: B. Siegel, Himelhoch's, Hudson's, and Harkness Pharmacy on the way home. The following Saturday, they planned a bus ride adventure to the downtown stores for some serious Christmas shopping, but this day was just for "bumming around," as they loved to put it. They stuffed what packages they could behind the seat, and what didn't fit, they simply held on their laps. They were in heaven! As they drove, they listened to their favorite radio station, WCAR, and sang and sang and sang. The Palermo girls were together again!

When they arrived home, they laughed and chattered their way through the kitchen to find their mother and show her all their "loot." She was in the den with Anne.

"Hi," Emma said, placing her packages on the floor.

"Hi, girls. Looks like you had some luck," their mother said, nodding at the bags. "Annie came over just now, Emma, to invite you to the football game tomorrow. Her whole family is going." Rosalie and Angela let out little gasps. Emma looked at them and then looked at Anne, now knowing what to say. *The girls must think this is a big deal,* Emma thought to herself.

"I told Annie that we would have to ask your father about this when he comes home tonight." Mother got up from the couch. "You can show me what you bought in a minute. I have to get Annie home. She can't stay for dinner with Tom and David home." Emma followed her and Anne to the door.

"Hey, Annie, did you play rummy with your brother yet?" Emma asked.

Anne turned and grinned. "Yeah, and I beat them, too!"

"Man, that's cool! Good for you. I hope I can go tomorrow," Emma said, not really convinced that she wanted to go to a pro football game on Thanksgiving.

Emma's mother took the coats from the closet and helped Anne with hers.

"The game is early. It starts at 12:30 because of Thanksgiving," Anne said as she slipped into her camel hair coat. Emma looked at her mother.

"We'll see," was all she would say. And with that they were out the door.

Emma stayed at the door and watched them go down the drive. *Do I really want to go to a Lions game and sit in that cold Briggs Stadium? It would be an awfully grown-up thing to do,* she thought.

Emma's father came home a bit early that evening, and they all sat down to eat. No one spoke much. Emma studied her father as she passed him the potatoes. He was frowning. *He must be tired.* Emma sighed. It was never a good idea to ask her father for anything when he was tired or hungry. But her mother jumped in with the hot topic, anyway.

"What do you think, Frank? Their whole family will be going, so Emma won't get lost or anything."

Poor Mother, Emma thought. *She's not headed in the right direction.* Emma knew that she would have to try another approach. "They probably want me to keep Annie company, Father. I'm sure she doesn't 'get' the game."

"Oh, and since *when* do you know so much about football, my dear?" Emma's father asked, unconvinced.

"Well, I watch it on TV with you, so I understand a little. Next fall, I get to cheerlead for Uncle Pete's Little League team, so I guess I know something." Emma had given it her best shot. She looked at her sisters for support. They were smiling, but said nothing, and the silence returned. Father was thinking. All you could hear was the clinking of the silverware against the dishes.

"We'll have to change our dinner time," he finally said. "Have you checked with your mother and Nona?" Emma held her breath and shot a glance at her mother and Nona. They were smiling and nodding.

"It's okay with them," Emma answered.

Emma's father put his fork down and looked at her. "Well, then, it's okay with me, too. Since you are too young to cook the turkey, I guess you can go with Annie."

Everyone at the table laughed, relieved. Emma beamed. "Oh, thank you, Father," she squeaked.

That night after saying good night to everyone, Emma crept into her parents' bedroom. When she was little, she had invented a private way of communicating with her father. She would hide little messages, on occasion, in his underwear drawer, sure he would find them on his way to his morning shower. That day, she placed a special "thank you" for him there, knowing that the next day, there would be no mention of the note—just a knowing glance from father to daughter.

It was their little secret. Then she returned to her own room, looking out for Rosalie and Angela. Giggling to herself, she turned out the nightstand lamp and crawled into bed. She hugged her pillow, closed her eyes, and thought, *Life is so good these days, and it seems to be getting better every day! God loves me for sure! Thank You, thank You.*

The next morning, the sun was out in full force, but Emma didn't know how to dress for the game. She put on her quilted robe and went downstairs. The house was already full of wonderful aromas, coming from the kitchen. Emma found her mother at her desk in the den.

"Morning, Mother," she said, rubbing the sleep from her eyes.

"Happy Thanksgiving, cutie. Rise and shine! Did you sleep well?" her mother asked.

Emma came up to her and leaned over her to give her a kiss. "Yup, I did." Emma noticed that her mother was wearing her new red dress, without the apron. She also had on the pair of triangle-shaped gold earrings, which had been a present from Nono Palermo. *She looks so pretty today! Maybe it's the red,* Emma thought. "I don't know how to dress for the game. I want to wear the new dress you bought me, but . . ."

"Why don't you wear it with a sweater and some knee socks? You can wear your good shoes, but you also have to wear your boots. That should keep you warm," her mother said as she turned back to her work on the desk.

"You think so?" Emma leaned over her mother's shoulder to see what it was that she was writing. *Oh, she's sending money to the missions again.* Emma wasn't surprised. Her mother had a soft heart for the missions, especially this time of year.

"Don't forget your hat and scarf and gloves," Emma's mother added.

"Can't I use my muff?" Emma owned a sweet white muff that she used for church during the winter.

"No, Emma, I'm afraid your muff is not very practical for a football game. Father will give you some money, and you can wrap it in your hanky and tuck it in your pocket."

Emma started to pout, but she caught herself. She would not pout today. Pouting was for babies, and she was doing grown-up things today. So pouting was out! Instead, she went to find some breakfast.

Three hours later, the entire Moreau family and Emma drove downtown to the game. Emma was amazed to see Mrs. Moreau wearing a fur coat, the color of her hair, to a football game! Anne sat next to her mother, looking content in her navy wool hat and coat. And Emma felt just as special in her pretty Sunday coat, with its fake fur collar and holiday corsage pinned neatly to it. Yes, Emma felt as festive as she looked.

"Have you been to many football games, Emma?" Mr. Moreau asked as he drove.

Hope my answer doesn't get me laughed at again, Emma thought. *Oh, well, I can't lie. Here goes.* "No, I've just been to my uncle's Little League games. He's a coach for the Spartans." Emma turned to face Anne. "Do you like football?" Anne just shrugged. Emma sat back in her seat. "I know a little, Annie. I'll help you." Anne then squeezed Emma's hand. Emma was delighted, for Anne rarely showed signs of affection. Emma was so pleased and proud to be sitting in this car, next to her little friend.

When they arrived at the parking lot, Mr. Moreau gave his keys to the attendant and then proceeded to help Mrs. Moreau and the girls from the car. "What a beautiful day!" He exclaimed. "And I am such a lucky man to be escorting all these beautiful ladies!" The girls giggled. "Why, just look at the two of you," he said as he took both their hands before crossing the street. "My little blonde Anne on my right, and her dear little shadow on my left. A man just couldn't get any luckier."

Emma looked up at him and thought, *Don't you have it backward?* But she smiled and kept walking, letting the comment pass.

Later, when the Palermos sat down for their Thanksgiving feast, Emma couldn't stop chattering. She tried to relay all the fun of her afternoon in one breath. The much-loved Detroit Lions had won the game over the Cleveland Browns.

"Did you know that they bring the popcorn and candy right there to you in the stand? And Mrs. Moreau actually ate a hot dog with me and Annie! The high school bands were huge, and they sounded great!"

All the family members had finished their dinners, and Emma realized everyone was staring at her, waiting for her to stop talking and finish hers. "I'm sorry I'm talking so much, but it was such fun! Thanks, Father, for letting me go." Emma turned her concentration to her food. Nona's fried potato balls were the best ever, but Emma was too excited to eat. She looked up at Angela and saw her looking rather gloomy. *Oh, she's jealous 'cause I got to go and she didn't. What was I supposed to do about that?* Emma sighed and went back to her food.

When the dinner was over, Emma got an idea. On Thanksgiving night, their tradition had always been to sing the first songs of the new Christmas season. So Emma thought she would start with one to cheer her sister. "Over the river and through the woods, to Grandmother's house we go. . . ." No one was joining in. "The horse knows the way, to carry the sleigh . . . hey!"

"What's going on?" Emma brought her pile of plates over to the kitchen sink, where Rosalie and Angela were standing. Rosalie looked like she was consoling Angela about something. *She looks like she is about to cry.* But Rosalie winked at Emma.

"I'm sorry I got invited instead of you, Angela." Emma didn't feel sorry at all, but she figured she had to say something.

"That's not what's wrong, Emma," Rosalie answered. "We're glad you got to go to the game."

"Then what's wrong?" Emma was confused.

"Oh, Angela here hasn't seen anything of David or Tom since they've been home."

"Was she supposed to?" Emma didn't have a clue when it came to boys.

"Not really." Angela sighed, turning on the faucets.

"I don't get it. This doesn't make sense."

"You're too young to understand," Angela replied as she started to line up the glasses.

Emma was hurt. *How can I be old enough to go to a football game but not old enough to "get" Angela's problem?* Emma went back to the dining room for more dishes, praying as she went, *God, please help me understand my sisters. I want to help them.* She picked up a bunch of silverware and started back for the kitchen when a light bulb went on in her brain. Her eyes opened wide. *This is brilliant!*

"Angela! I have an idea, I think. Mother wants someone to bring the Moreaus some pheasant on Saturday so they can have a taste. She knows I was planning on going over there to teach Annie a new game. I can tell her I can't handle the food without spilling it, and you can come with me! The boys might be hanging around, and then you might see them! Emma was ecstatic and plunked the silverware onto the counter for emphasis.

A smile crept over Angela's face. "I guess that might work. Okay." And she proceeded to squeeze Joy all over the glasses.

"Good! Now can we start singing? Let's do Mother's and Father's favorite," Emma suggested. And so they did. "In old Judea, amidst the plains afar . . ." Their voices were loud and strong. They wanted to make sure they could be heard in the next room, where they knew their parents were waiting. The harmony of their sweet notes filled the air, leaving no room for any kind of sadness.

CHAPTER THIRTEEN

HELPING OUT

On Saturday morning, Emma stationed herself at Rosalie's front bedroom window, peeking through the drapes and acting as Angela's "lookout," just like in the cowboy movies. Angela was in the bathroom fussing with her hair. "Has anyone left the house yet?" she asked. "No, no one. Not all morning." Emma was growing impatient. "Are you almost done in there?"

"Yes, yes. I'm coming. Just one more barrette. Oh, I'm so nervous. I hope I look all right." Angela came into Rosalie's room to snatch some perfume from the dressing table. "What do you think?" she asked her baby sister. Angela looked lovely in her matching skirt and sweater.

Emma closed the drapes and gave her sister a critical look. *She looks so old! It must be the red lipstick.* "You look really nice, and you're lucky Father isn't home. He'd never let you leave the house with that lipstick on." Angela just giggled and took a last look out the window.

"Come on," Emma said, "I can tell by the smell that the food must be ready. Remember, I'm going over there to help Annie learn to play Clue. So I won't be able to baby-sit you." This didn't seem to phase Angela one bit.

"Oh, that's fine," Angela said, inspecting her nails. "You can run along, and I'll just chat a while with Mary or Madelaine about the pheasant if the boys aren't home. And if they are, I'll just stay and chat with them awhile." She seemed pleased with her plan. After checking her hair in the vanity mirror one last time, the two girls went downstairs.

"I don't know why we have to go through all of this," Emma sighed as she descended the stairs. *I sure hope this doesn't get me in any trouble!*

Their mother met them in the foyer, holding a large CorningWare pot with two big potholders. She waited for them to put on their coats. "Be very careful with this, girls. Do watch where you step." Emma shook her head as she put on her red pea jacket. "I can't carry that, Mother, without spilling," she said, eyeing the food.

"Well, that's what you have a big sister for," her mother replied, smiling. Emma wanted to laugh out loud—*Who's helping whom here?*—but she didn't. She just gave her sister a "look." Angela giggled again, as she took the sturdy pot from her mother. Angela's eyes opened wide. "Wow, this is heavy!"

"Have you got a firm hold there, dear? I don't want you to drop it halfway there," their mother asked, a bit worried.

"Yes, I'm pretty sure I do. You can let go. We'll be back soon," Angela reassured her.

"You'll be back soon," Emma corrected. "It might take me a while to teach Annie that game."

Their mother opened the door for the girls. "Be careful on the steps." They stepped out into the cold morning air. The snow had melted, and the sun was bright in the blue sky.

"We will," they answered, inching their way down the drive. Their mother watched them for a minute and then returned to her warm kitchen.

"Let me do the talking," Angela instructed, concentrating on the dish in front of her.

"What is it with you?" Emma was amused at her sister's attitude. "I talk to David all the time. Besides, I'm just going to go in and find Annie, remember?"

"Okay. That's fine, I guess." Angela's eyes were still on the pot.

She is really nervous. Probably because she's never been in their house before. Please God, don't let her drop the food! And please let one of the boys be home, Emma prayed.

A few minutes later, the two girls were ringing the doorbell. Mary answered in her cheerful way. "Well, what do we have here? Miss Emma from across the street and one of her lovely sisters, I presume. Come in, come in, ladies." Mary led them into the bright breakfast room. "Look here, master David, the charming Palermo girls have come bearing gifts." She left the girls standing in the doorway. David was sitting at the table alone, eating a sandwich. He got up to greet them.

"Hello, there. Come in," David said, wiping his mouth.

"Hello, David. This is my sister Angela. She's brought some pheasant for you all to try. Our Uncle Louie went hunting and caught three. Mother cooked it this morning," Emma said, staying in the doorway.

"Nice to meet you, Angela. That's great of you. I don't think I've ever had pheasant before." He was smiling his most engaging smile. "I was just having some lunch. Did you have yours yet?"

"Oh, we ate a while ago," Angela said, setting the heavy pot down on the table.

"Well, how about a Coke?" he offered.

"Oh, that would be nice," Angela was blushing as she smiled and sat down.

"Not for me," Emma said. "I have to go find Annie. Promised I'd teach her another game."

"Yeah, and thanks for teaching her rummy," David said in mock disgust. "That's all she wants to do now is beat her poor defenseless brother."

Emma grinned as she turned to leave. She never thought that she could beat David at anything. And with Anne, somehow she had. "See you later." And off she went down the hall.

She found Anne in her bedroom sitting on the soft green carpet, trying to set up the game pieces. "Hi," Emma said, entering the room.

"Hi," Anne replied. "I don't know what to do with all this stuff." The "weapons" lay in a pile to one side. The papers and pencils were in front of her. "I'll show you," Emma said, sitting down and sorting everything. There was a long pause. Then Emma had to ask, "Does David have a girlfriend?" She didn't look up, but kept sorting the pieces.

"Not here," Anne said, watching Emma put all the "weapons" in their "rooms."

"What do you mean, 'not here'? Does he have one at school?" Emma kept sorting.

"No. Not there, either."

Emma stopped and looked up, "Then where?"

"At the cottage," Anne said, not even blinking.

"Oh." Emma hadn't thought about that. *I'm going to have to warn Angela. Why do I feel like some kind of spy?* she wondered. But she straightened up and smiled at Anne. *I am here to have some fun with Annie.* "Let's start," she said. "Whom do you want to be, Miss Scarlet or Professor Plum?"

When evening came, Emma and Rosalie put on their dungarees and head kerchiefs and headed for the basement for some fun, but dusty, work. Thanksgiving was officially over, and it was time to hunt for the Christmas decorations. The musty storage room held many treasures: their father's sketchbooks and charcoals, old leather suitcases, vintage wine bottles for special occasions, and many other great things. But that night, the search was on for some specific boxes, and Emma was sure she knew where they would be found. Removing the tape from the cartons, the girls started sifting through sheets of tissue paper for the delicate items.

"That was nice of you today," Rosalie said as she pulled out a tiny ornament.

"What was nice?" Emma asked, only half listening. She had uncovered a bunch of Italian lights.

"What you did for Angela today. David probably has girlfriends all over the place, but at least she got to talk to him a little."

"Oh, that." Emma would never understand what all the fuss was about, but she knew she wanted to help her sisters if she could. "I really did promise to teach Annie that game. There's not much time for stuff like that when school's on."

Rosalie put her big box of glass ornaments down on the floor. They were beautiful, and some of them were very old. She picked up a small red bell with its paint nearly gone and stared at it.

"Be careful with that one," Emma warned as she looked up from her pile of lights. "That was Mother's when she was little, remember?" Rosalie nodded. She did indeed remember, for this was the very ornament the girls first searched for each year, to keep it from getting broken. Rosalie carefully set it aside on a shelf, out of harm's way. Then she started in on another box.

"You've been really good for Annie, Emma. Has anyone told you?" Emma just smiled, pleased with the compliment. "You think so?"

"Yes, I know so. Everyone says so. Look at what you tried to do for her today!"

"Oh, Rosalie, this is a mess," Emma cried out.

Rosalie looked over at her sister and laughed. Emma was covered with light strands. "Do you want some help with those? Here, let's bring them all into the rec room. We can turn on some music and stretch the lines across the floor."

Rosalie untangled Emma, and they carried their boxes into the next room. Emma pulled out more strands of lights, and Rosalie turned on "Winter Wonderland." Emma sang the melody, and Rosalie harmonized. "Sleigh bells ring, are you listening? In the lane, snow is glistening...."

The music continued, but Emma wanted to keep talking about Anne. "The problem I have with Annie is that a lot of times, I feel like she doesn't understand a word I'm saying. You know?"

"Yes, I think I know what you mean. But she probably understands a whole lot more than you think." There were lights now all across the floor.

"Like today," Emma went on, "that game was way too hard for her, but she really wanted to keep trying, over and over again. I was losing my temper and my patience—don't tell mother, please. And Annie sat there all confused. I felt really terrible." Emma surveyed the floor.

"What a mess of lights!" she said as she went to plug them all in.

"Watch where you step, kiddo," Rosalie warned. "You don't want to get lit up like a Christmas tree." Emma smiled at her sister's weak joke. "Speaking of Christmas trees, you won't be able to help us pick one out this year, will you?" As soon as those words fell out of her mouth, Emma wanted them back. *Oh, why did I have to remind her? Ooooo, that was so dumb!*

Trying to cover her mistake, she quickly added, "It's so nice that you can help with these decorations, though."

Rosalie kept her head down. She didn't need reminding that she would be gone for the annual Christmas tree hunt. "Well, I can get you guys started at least with the decoration business. You and Angela will have to finish next week 'cause my train leaves tomorrow at three." She tried to sound positive.

"I know. I miss you already," Emma said, her smile fading.

"And don't forget, Uncle Johnny will be here soon to put up the outdoor lights, too!"

Emma brightened at the thought. Christmas was coming, and that meant her sister Rosalie would come home again, this time for a nice long vacation.

CHAPTER FOURTEEN

LIKE ONE OF THE FAMILY

December on Oxford Road. Oh, how Emma loved it, especially when it snowed! The street curved here and there, giving the feeling of being on a country lane. Emma felt that way now as her mother drove her home from school. When they came up the driveway, Emma let out a squeal. "Ooooooo, Mother, look!" There on a ladder up ahead was Uncle Johnny, just as Rosalie had predicted a few days before. He was busy tying the long green garlands to their balcony railing.

"Oh, Mother, please let me out here. I want to watch Uncle for a minute." Mother stopped the car, and Emma jumped out. She stood and waved at her uncle as her mother drove to the garage. Uncle Johnny turned his head at last and waved back. "Hello, nina," he yelled.

"Hi, Uncle Johnny! It looks so pretty!" Emma yelled back.

"I call you when it's done, okay? You can do the lights."

"Oh, yes, yes!" Emma shrieked, jumping up and down. *This is just the best time of the year! I love it, I love it, I love it!*

Then she ran into the house. The girls only had a half day of school that day, and their mother had given them "kitchen privileges" so they could do some Christmas baking. She knew Angela would already be inside waiting for her. Emma's mouth began to water as she thought about the yummy butter cookies they would cut out and decorate. Anne would be coming to help as well.

"Oh, it is so neat outside!" Emma announced as she came through the garage side door, stomping the snow off her galoshes. "Uncle Johnny said I could go out later, when he's done, and turn on all the lights!"

"We know. Mother told us." Angela's voice came from around the corner. Emma hung up her coat and hat, sniffling from the cold, and went to the kitchen. When she reached the doorway, she stopped. "You started without me," she whined.

Angela, clad in one of Nona's big flowered aprons, stood at the counter, measuring milk, and right next to her was Anne, dressed the same, sifting flour into the big yellow bowl. "We couldn't wait forever," Angela said. "You know Mother. She wants to get back in here by four o'clock to make dinner, so we can't fool around."

Emma opened the pantry to get her apron and searched the pockets for a Kleenex. After wiping her nose, she went to the big kitchen drawer to look for the cookie cutters. "Here, Annie, come pick out the ones you want to use. I want to make a lot of Santa faces this year."

"You only pick Santa faces because they use up the dough faster," Angela said, trying to keep the flour out of her hair.

"Well, that will get us out of the kitchen faster, won't it, sister dear?" Emma gave Angela a smug look, then walked to the sink to wash her hands. The girls found some Christmas music on the radio and sang as they worked.

Soon the smell of cinnamon filled the air. Mother inhaled approvingly as she came to check on the girls' progress.

"Sure smells like Christmas. Sure looks like Christmas," their mother said, smiling. The girls grinned at her with their flour-smudged faces. "But now it's time to clean up," their mother added. The girls looked around at the mess they had created. The fun was over.

The girls' mother turned to Anne. "You can wait in the den, Annie, after you wash up." Emma and Angela objected. "Oh, no," they wailed. "She made this mess, too. She has to stay and help!"

Anne just shrugged. "I don't mind helping," she said.

"Guess you're not company anymore, Annie," Emma's mother said. "Just don't tell Mary we put you to work over here." They all laughed.

The days grew shorter and colder. The first day of vacation arrived, and with it, more snow. Emma was so excited that she jumped out of bed at her usual time, rather than try to sleep in. She threw on her robe and pulled open her drapes so she could catch the scene below her windows.

It was a winter wonderland for sure. The patio wore a white blanket, and the fruit trees looked like little guards in snow white uniforms. The flakes covered everything and were still flurrying everywhere. "Oh, does that look cool!" Emma said, putting on her slippers. She made a dash for the front staircase, hoping no one would catch her as she flew down to the foyer. Then she slid across the shiny marble and landed in the kitchen with a thud, startling her mother.

"Oh, Mother, look at all the snow!" Emma said. She pointed to the window.

"Good morning to you, too, dear. Yes, there's lots of it, I'm afraid," her mother answered as she poured café au lait into her breakfast bowl. "Ready for some breakfast on your first day of 'freedom'?"

"Oh, I just have to see first," Emma said, pressing her nose against the window. "The snow makes everything sparkle so."

"Yes, it does look glittery out there. God is quite an artist. Come sit. I'll make you some toast."

Emma did as she was told. She loved dunking her buttered toast into her hot milk and coffee. But first she said a prayer out loud. "Thank you, God, for the food and the snow and for bringing Rosalie home tomorrow. Amen."

"Yes," Emma's mother said. "She'll be home with us for almost three weeks. Imagine that!" Her mother smiled as she brought the food to the table.

Emma hummed as she ate. She was so overjoyed that morning. Life couldn't get much better.

"Are you and Annie going to make a snowman today?"

Emma swallowed her food and thought about this. "Do you think her parents let her play in the snow?" Emma asked as she blew on her hot coffee. "Oh, I don't know why she couldn't," Emma's mother said, slicing a banana for them to share.

"What happens if she gets wet?" Emma asked, with toast in her mouth.

"Well, what do we do with you when you get wet?"

Emma giggled. "You bring me inside and make me change my socks." She went back to humming and thinking about the days ahead. *They are going to be so great! What, with Christmas caroling and visiting my cousins and Midnight Mass—it's all too cool!*

Her mother interrupted her thoughts, "When you're finished eating, you can call Annie and see if she can play in the snow. Tell her to bundle up well."

"Okay," Emma said, and she got up to clear her dishes, still humming.

An hour later, Emma dressed to go outside. She pulled her leggings over her corduroys, buckled up her galoshes, buttoned her jacket, and wrapped her muffler around her neck. Then she tied on her white angora hat and pulled on her blue mittens. She could barely move. *Sure hope I'm not forgetting anything!* she thought. Clapping her hands together, she waddled to the front door to wait for Anne.

As she looked through the small window, she spotted the postman trudging up the drive. This was his first delivery of the day. With the Christmas cards flooding the mail these days, he would be back for another delivery in the afternoon. Emma opened the door to receive their bundle. "Thank you, and merry Christmas!" she called. He waved and turned toward the Moreaus'.

Emma noticed David and Tom throwing snowballs at each other in their front yard. *Where is Annie?* she wondered. She was getting warm standing there in all those clothes. *Oh, I'm not waiting anymore,* she decided. And she opened the door and went out, swishing down the drive, her boots kicking up mounds of snow.

At the curb, Emma stopped to watch the Moreau boys battle each other. David was taller and faster, so it looked like he was winning. But they both were covered with snow. She laughed and waved at them. They waved back. *This sure is different from last June. Was it only last June that I met these guys? Seems like a million years ago.*

"Where's your sister?" Emma yelled.

"She's in the house. She should be out soon," David said. But Annie was sneaking up behind David with a huge snowball aimed at his head.

SPLAT! Bull's-eye! "Oooooo," Emma squealed. David let out a howl and spun around to catch the culprit, expecting one of his brothers. But it was Anne standing there, laughing.

"I'll get you, Annie," he teased, and pretended to chase her. *He forgot she's not supposed to run!* Emma tore across the street to come to Anne's aid. Anne continued to throw more snow and didn't seem to need much help, though. Tom stood where he was and laughed. His big brother was getting pelted by two little girls!

"I give, I give!" David yelped, falling to the ground as if mortally wounded. Cautiously, Anne walked over to her brother, with more "ammunition" ready, just in case. Emma watched her, and then, SWAT! Tom had hurled a big, mushy glop of snow at her, and it landed right in her face!

Whoa! Emma was startled. She wanted to laugh and cry, but she could do neither. The snow was in her eyes, up her nose, in her hair, and in her mouth—just everywhere! *"Oh, what did he have to go and do that for? I know he was defending his brother, but . . ."* she thought as she pushed the snow from her eyes.

Tom came running over to see if Emma was okay. "Are you all right?" he asked, brushing the snow off her hat. "I'm really sorry if I hurt you." "Oh, I'm okay. You were just having some fun, I know," Emma replied, spitting snow. "My mother says I'm tough—I won't melt. But you guys are kinda dangerous. I only came over here to make a snowman with Annie. Want to help?" She bit her lip. *Did I just say that? I asked a boy to do something with me?* She was amazing herself these days.

"Another time. Dave and I have to go and get haircuts. The snow's pretty good, though, as you can see," Tom said, and as he smiled, his china blue eyes lit up with mischief. Emma smiled, too, and brushed off the remaining snow as she walked over to where Anne was standing.

"Where do you want to build the snowman?" Emma asked.

"Here." Anne said, and she went right to work. This was one game she didn't need to be told how to play.

"Have you guys got a carrot and a broom we can use?" Emma asked David. *I did it again! Where am I getting the nerve?* Blushing, Emma bent to pile up the snow for Anne, not waiting for David's answer.

"I don't know, but we'll go check." Dave and Tom turned for the house. "Good luck."

The girls worked at a steady pace, and Mr. Snowman came together in no time. He stood about four feet high and was on the slim side for a snowman. The boys never did come back outside, so Emma searched for twigs and stones to make his face come alive. Thirty minutes later, they stood back to admire their handiwork. Emma noticed Anne smiling. *She does that a lot these days.*

"He's pretty cool. Think your parents will like him?" Emma asked, clapping her hands together.

"Hope so. I have to go in now and wrap some presents," Anne said.

"You do?" Emma started to get excited in spite of her frozen fingers. "I love to wrap gifts. Can I help?"

"Sure." And the two girls left Mr. Snowman to amuse himself.

"My, my, and what do we have here?" Mary asked, opening the door. "A couple of frozen maids in from the hinterland, it looks like. Come in, come in, and get those wet things off. You can hang them on the chairs in the breakfast room. I'll have Madelaine make you some nice hot cocoa. It'll be just a minute." And she went to find Madelaine.

Well, it will take more than a minute to get all these clothes off! Emma thought as she pulled off her boots. Emma felt odd padding around the Moreau home in her stocking feet. *Hope Mrs. Moreau isn't home.*

"Come, come, the Mrs. won't mind," Mary said, reading Emma's thoughts. "Let's put those socks in the oven for a wee bit." That got Emma's attention. *She wants to put my socks where?* But Mary was insisting. "Come, come, Emma from across the street; off with those wet socks, darlings." Mary was opening the oven door and adjusting the temperature dial. "I'll just put them in here for a few minutes while you two drink your chocolate." There was no arguing with Mary. The girls handed over their socks and made a beeline back to the breakfast room, where they quickly sat down and hid their feet under the table.

"Does she always put socks in the oven?" Emma whispered. Anne giggled. "Only once in a while. The clothes dryer is way down in the basement." This arrangement seemed to make sense to Anne, so Emma just wondered about other things. "Where do you wrap your presents? We use the spare bedroom over the garage."

Madelaine arrived with their steaming mugs. "Here you are, my two *femmes des neige* (snow maidens), chocolate to warm you, *n'est-ce pas* (isn't that so)?"

Emma smiled at her and said, "Thank you," not understanding a word. After Madelaine left, Anne answered Emma's question, "We keep all the wrapping things in the guest room next to mine. Mother has lots of pretty bows and ribbons and paper, too. I don't make very good bows." Anne frowned.

"Oh, that's okay. I'm great at making bows," Emma bragged, swinging her bare feet and sipping her drink. She didn't realize how her comment sounded. Anne looked intently at her.

"You're so good at everything," she said with a wistful voice. Emma stopped drinking. Her face went red as feelings of guilt flooded over her. Her mother's words about "trying" came to her now. She had to say something nice to make Anne feel better.

"Well, I only know how to make bows because Angela taught me. And she had to show me many, many times. It is a little tricky, but I can teach you." Emma hoped she sounded reassuring. *Please, God, help her to feel better. Help me to show her how to make bows*, she prayed.

Anne's face brightened. "We have a radio up there. We can listen to Christmas music."

"Good. Are you finished with your chocolate?"

"Yup." Anne got up from her chair.

"Hope our socks are done, too!" Emma joked as she and Anne gathered their mugs and spoons. They made their way back to the kitchen and brought their things to the sink. Anne went to retrieve the socks. Madelaine was busy preparing a roast for the evening meal. She looked up at the girls as they approached. "Already fini?"

"How do you say 'very good' in French?" Emma asked her.

"*C'est tres bon.*" Madelaine was pleased Emma wanted to use French.

"Well, *c'est tres bon*, Madelaine. Thank you." Emma tried to mimic Madelaine's accent. "You mean 'merci,' don't you?" Madelaine asked. "Okay, merci," Emma added.

"*C'est rien, ma cherie*" (It is nothing, my dear).

Emma looked puzzled by this last phrase, and Madelaine laughed. "Go, you two. I have to finish now—shoo!" She waved them away.

"We are going to make pretty presents," Anne announced.

"Beautiful presents," Emma corrected as they headed for the hall.

CHAPTER FIFTEEN

THE GIFT OPENED

"Christmas Eve, Christmas Eve, Oh, how I love Christmas Eve," Emma sang as she moved through the house. She had a talent for turning phrases into songs, and at this time of year, it was such an easy thing to do! She couldn't help herself. Music was everywhere!

Now she headed for the best room of the house. They called it the "lounge," and it was special, for besides being shaped like a horseshoe, hundreds of small, louvered windows made up its walls. Currently, the grand spruce Christmas tree resided there, so at night, when it was all lit up, the tree sent Palermo Christmas greetings to all the neighbors!

Emma stood in front of the tree to admire her work. It smelled so good! And she felt responsible for almost every ornament, light bulb, and wearisome strand of tinsel it wore! "TA DA!" she sang as she plugged in the lights.

"Emma, go get changed," her mother called from the next room, bringing her back to reality. "Nona and Nono Palermo will be here soon."

"Okay," Emma answered. No one had to ask her twice that night! It was Christmas Eve, and she had a beautiful velvet jumper to put on, as well as new Mary Janes. So she flew up the stairs, her soaring spirits lifting her along. "Here I come, Mary Janes, here I come!" she sang.

Thirty minutes later, she came back down the stairs, feeling like a fairy princess. She stopped in the front hall to check her reflection in the big hall mirror. After adjusting her hair bow, she went to find her father.

"Wow!" he exclaimed when she walked into the den. "Look at our little Christmas Carol!" Now, Emma didn't particularly like the Christmas Carol person down at Hudson's Toyland, for she wore a scary-looking black patent leather wig and was snippy with the children who came to visit Santa. But Emma knew her father was only trying to pay her a compliment, so she curtsied and said, "Merci. That's French! I like your vest, too."

"Well, Mademoiselle, we seem to be the only two ready. Shall we go and try out Nona's eggnog?" Her father bent low to offer Emma his arm. She giggled. *This is going to be a great night!* she thought.

Everyone finally arrived, bringing presents galore! After taking their coats, Emma's father and Emma ushered them all into the living room to enjoy a family holiday toast by the blazing fire. Rosalie sat down at the piano and played "O Holy Night," and everyone clapped. Then Emma's mother invited them to come into the dining room. There were candles everywhere, casting a warm glow on all who entered. Emma couldn't help but smile at her family, so festive in their Christmas finery. And the food!

It was too pretty to eat! The silver platters of roast beef and ravioli looked like they had jumped out of a magazine. Even Nona Palermo's fish dishes almost looked appetizing. They were one tradition Emma could do without. She knew she would have to have a taste, but she just picked at her food. She wanted to get on with the fun.

The gifts were waiting, and Mass was to follow. This would be Emma's first Midnight Mass, and she couldn't wait to see how the Ladies of the Altar Society had decorated the church.

Why are they taking so long to drink their coffee? Emma was about to burst. She looked at Rosalie, so pretty in her taffeta dress, and Rosalie smiled back. She knew what Emma was thinking, so she slowly got up and addressed her father. "Emma and I are going to go sort the gifts now so we can get started in a few minutes."

That Rosalie is so smart, Emma thought, following her out of the room. Their mother and Nona were already in the kitchen putting the food away, and Angela was clearing the plates.

I hope Father takes the hint.

An hour later, the lounge was full of people, presents, and piles of paper and ribbons. "Oooo, I love my new pajamas! I love my new desk set! I love my new perfume! I love all my presents! Thank you, thank you, thank you, everyone!" Emma gushed as she bounced from one family member to another, doling out kisses as she went. Mother started to pick up some of the wrappings and bows. She noticed Emma's level of excitement reaching a fever pitch. "Emma, calm down, dear, and go get ready for church now. We want to get there early to find seats and hear the choir."

"Okay, okay," Emma said, moving over the piles of boxes.

"Say good-bye to Nona and Nono because they are going home now," Emma's mother continued. Her youngest child never ceased to amaze her—so responsible one moment, and such a little girl the next.

The girls' father went to get his parents' coats, and Emma followed them all to the front door. "Oh, good-bye, good-bye! And merry Christmas!" she squealed. Nona Palermo, who was only as tall as Emma, beamed at her granddaughter and pinched her cheek, the Italian way.

"Buon Natale, benedetta" (Merry Christmas, little blessed one), Nona said. Emma smiled back. She needed no translation.

The parking lot was filling up, even though Mass would not start for another hour. "Wish we could get some fresh snow," Emma said as she hurried her mother and father along.

"Emma, stop tugging," her mother said. "We'll be inside soon enough." Emma did slow down, and when she reached the great wooden doors of the ancient church, she stopped.

She wanted to savor every bit of the scene before her, so she took her time entering.

And when she did, her eyes lit up with joy at the sight of the sanctuary. It was filled with evergreens, all ablaze with tiny white lights. The candles, held aloft by their giant gold candlesticks, added warmth and majesty to the holy place. "Oh, how beautiful!" Emma whispered loudly. "Look at the manger! By St. Joseph! It's as big as I am!" She turned around to look at the trimmed wreaths, which seemed to be everywhere. "Aren't they pretty? The bows look like lace!" Emma was awed. "We see, dear," her father answered as he guided them to a pew. "Oh, please, please, Father, can we sit closer, just for tonight? I want to see everything!" Emma pleaded, grabbing his arm. "Oh, sure. Go ahead a few," he said. But Emma marched right to the very middle of the church and walked in, hoping the rest of her family was following.

She knew she was expected to kneel, but she couldn't stop looking around. There was so much to see! The altar servers were all dressed in red and white. *How cool! They even look like Christmas!* she thought. Turning to face the back, she looked up and saw the members of the choir getting their music ready. Their black robes were decorated with red carnations. She waited for them to start. "Oh, come, all ye faithful, joyful and triumphant . . ." Emma hummed along. She loved this carol and sang it in Latin as well.

"Sit down," her mother whispered to her. Emma knelt, though, and bowed her head to pray. *Oh, thank You, Lord, for this wonderful moment. Thank You for my beautiful presents and my family and friends and especially for my new friend, Annie. . . . Thank You for helping me learn how to play with her and be her friend. . . . Amen.*

Raising her head, Emma saw some of the Moreau family filing into a pew near the front. Anne, Carter, and Larry were missing. This made Emma sad for a moment. She wished her little friend were here to share this joyous night. *This beautiful, holy night,* Emma thought and said another prayer: *Thank You, God, for helping Annie learn more so we can do more together. Amen.* Nona said her rosary beads and stared at Emma. Emma smiled at her and opened her hymnal.

Two hours later, it was a very sleepy Emma that her mother walked back to the car. "Well, you stayed awake, anyway," her mother said, but Emma only yawned.

"Wasn't it just wonderful? Wasn't it magical?" Emma said, yawning.

Her father started up the car. "I'll have you all warm in a jiffy."

"Oh, look, everyone," Angela cried from the back seat, "it's snowing again."

"Just like in the movies," Rosalie added as she climbed in back with her.

Sitting in front, Emma leaned against her mother. She loved to nuzzle the big fox fur collar on her mother's coat. "It's been such a glorious night," she said in muffled tones. Her mother gazed down at her. "Well, dear, for you, it's been quite a year, don't you think?"

"Why?"

"Well, just think about it."

"Oh, mother, I'm too tired," Emma yawned again.

"You did so many grown-up things this year, didn't you?"

"Yeah, I guess I did. I got grown-up gifts, too."

Silent night, holy night. No one spoke a word. The windshield wipers swished, and the car tires crunched the new snow. Her mother had to answer her own question.

"Your greatest gift this year was probably Annie, don't you think? All the grown-up things you did this year you did because of Annie. You went to that big football game. You got over your fear of overnights. You helped her learn to sing and dance and play games, not to mention helping with homework. I'd say you did some amazing things this year, and all because of that one little girl, your friend Annie."

Emma's father turned slowly down Oxford Road. The trees all glistened in the light of the street lamps. All was calm, all was bright.

Emma was awake. She started thinking again about that day last June—that very hot day when she didn't want to have anything to do with the strange little girl from across the street. Once again, Emma knew her mother was right.

"I didn't realize she was a gift," Emma admitted softly.

"Do you realize it now?" her mother asked.

"Yes, I guess I do."

"Well, then, merry Christmas, Emma."

Sleep in heavenly peace.

QUESTIONS FOR DISCUSSION

CHAPTER ONE:

1. Why is Emma so disturbed about meeting her new neighbor?
2. What is it about Annie's home life that leaves us surprised?
3. What is it about Annie that makes Emma think she is bored all the time?
4. Why does Emma think she could impress Annie by bringing her to Rosalie's room?

CHAPTER TWO:

1. Why does Emma think her social life is a "disaster"?
2. Why does Emma consider Annie to be so different?
3. What explanation does Emma's mother give her concerning Annie?
4. Emma's mother tells her there is a key to understanding Annie. What is it?
5. How does Emma try to get God's attention in church?

CHAPTER THREE:

1. What does Emma find when she bravely marches over to the Moreau home?
2. What is so amazing about Annie's bedroom?
3. Why is Emma impressed with Mrs. Moreau? How is she different from Mrs. Palermo?

CHAPTER FOUR:

1. Why does Emma panic when Annie's brothers arrive?
2. What happens when their tour of Oxford Road is finished?
3. Why does Emma think it is so hard to be with Annie?
4. What does this tell you about Emma and her notion of friendship?

CHAPTER FIVE:

1. Emma has another problem with Annie that she needs to discuss with her mother. What is it?
2. What is Emma's mother's suggestion?
3. Rosalie intervenes with a solution. What is it?
4. How does Emma feel when everyone gushes over Annie?
5. What does Emma's father tell her about Annie? How does Emma respond?

CHAPTER SIX:

1. Emma gets caught in a social blunder. What solution does her mother offer?
2. How does Emma feel about her Nona?

Annie's Song

3. How does Annie react to Nona?
4. What are Nona's comments to the three sisters after dinner? Is she right?

CHAPTER SEVEN:

1. Emma has a big hang-up that causes her to miss out on fun. What is it?
2. Emma expresses her fears about the upcoming school year. What are they about?
3. How does she console herself about the days ahead?

CHAPTER EIGHT:

1. Why is Emma so cranky with her mother?
2. Her mother reminds Emma of something regarding Annie. What is it?
3. Rosalie wants something from Emma. What is it?
4. How does Emma respond?
5. At the Moreau home, Emma feels like she has been transported to the movies. What does she see?
6. Mrs. Moreau asks for a favor, and Emma panics. Why?
7. What magical thing happens then?
8. How does Emma fulfill her part of Rosalie's deal?
9. What is the awful news Emma has to deliver to Angela?

CHAPTER NINE:

1. School has started, and Emma runs into a conflict. What is it?
2. How does her mother console her? What is Nona's suggestion?
3. Mary also has words of advice. What are they?

4. What is Nona's bit of wisdom for Emma and Angela?

CHAPTER TEN:

1. Emma is still frustrated with Annie. What does Emma want to do?
2. Emma wants her mother to change her clothes. Why?
3. Mrs. Moreau's invitation presents a huge problem. What is it?
4. Why is Emma unhappy with her new social life?
5. How does the problem get resolved?

CHAPTER ELEVEN:

1. How does Emma turn Annie into a "little monster"?
2. Why does Emma get to go to the train station? What does she see?
3. Emma thinks Rosalie has changed. Has she? How?
4. Rosalie thinks Emma has changed. Has she? How? What about the way she talks?

CHAPTER TWELVE:

1. Why is there a fuss about the football game?
2. What is the little secret Emma shares with her father?
3. Of the two young girls, who is really the "little shadow"?
4. Why does Angela still pout at dinner? What does Emma offer to do? What does this prove about Emma?
5. What traditional thing do the girls do after supper?

CHAPTER THIRTEEN:

1. Emma wants to help Angela, but she feels like a spy. Why?
2. Rosalie pays Emma a big compliment. What is it?
3. Emma puts her foot in her mouth when sorting the ornaments. What does she say?

CHAPTER FOURTEEN:

1. There is a "silent" character in the story. What is it?
2. How is Annie made to feel just like one of the family?
3. Emma surprises herself by doing what?
4. Emma brags and causes a problem. How?

CHAPTER FIFTEEN:

1. Emma loves everything about Christmas Eve. How so?
2. What does Emma do at church?
3. After Mass, Emma's mother brings home the truth to Emma. What is it?